Fruit on the Table

Seasonal recipes from the Green Apron kitchen

About the Author

Born in Detroit and raised in Co. Clare, Theresa Storey now lives in rural Co. Limerick, where she puts her botany degree to good use growing fruit and vegetables and managing the family orchards, gardens and woodland. She uses the fruit of her labour to make fabulous preserves for her company The Green Apron, which has won many national and international food awards. She also teaches sustainable living, blogs and tries to keep up with her three kids.

Fruit on the Table

Seasonal recipes from the Green Apron kitchen

Theresa Storey

THE O'BRIEN PRESS
DUBLIN

First published 2016 by
The O'Brien Press Ltd,
12 Terenure Road East, Rathgar, Dublin 6, D06 HD27, Ireland.
Tel: +353 1 4923333; Fax: +353 1 4922777
E-mail: books@obrien.ie. Website: www.obrien.ie

The O'Brien Press is a member of Publishing Ireland.

ISBN: 978-1-84717-777-3

Photography by Valerie O'Connor
Photographs by Theresa Storey: pp. 12, 51 (except for top right and centre),
57, 72 (top left, centre right, bottom three), 86, 110, 126, 136, 140, 150, 172, 180, 187
Photograph on p. 140, centre, by Mike Cosgrave
Front cover photograph courtesy of Shutterstock

Design and layout by Tanya M. Ross www.elementinc.ie

1 3 5 4 2
16 18 20 19 17

Printed by EDELVIVES, Spain
The paper in this book is produced using pulp from managed forests

Published in

DUBLIN
UNESCO
City of Literature

Contents

PRESERVING

Introduction

Most of my early memories revolve around food and using the harvest. My family moved to Ireland from Detroit when I had just turned six so I don't have very many memories of the USA, but I do remember that Mom and Dad used to go to the farmers' market early on summer Saturday mornings, buy bushels of whichever produce was in season and then preserve it for later use. Corn, beans, tomatoes, blueberries – all got canned. I remember helping Mom to make jar after jar of spiced blueberries, the kitchen smelling of cinnamon and cloves and all our hands stained purple with berry juice. In the autumn, Mom would take the sisters and me to the apple farm and pick up baskets of apples, fresh juice and doughnuts.

In the 1970s, my parents bought a small farm in Co. Clare where we grew our own fruit and vegetables, kept chickens, ducks, geese, donkeys, sheep and cows. We were almost entirely self-sufficient for food. In the middle of winter we ate all our own peas, beans, cabbages, carrots and potatoes, we had our own apples until Easter, and every day we ate jam made from fruit we'd picked ourselves, from the garden or the hedge. Mom and Dad also brought our produce into the Limerick market every week. Our stall sold vegetables, plants, preserves, baked goods and crafts. We grew and sold some more unusual vegetables (for the time) such as mangetout, asparagus peas and Swiss chard, and we had the first pumpkins and squash ever seen in Clare or Limerick. That's probably what triggered my love of plants and why I studied Botany in university.

I'm far from being self-sufficient (it's just too much hard work, and, what's more, my husband and children mutinied), but I do grow much of my own fruit and vegetables at our farmhouse and in my parents' walled gardens in west Co. Limerick. I've continued on the family business and can be found every Saturday in the Milk Market in Limerick city selling our fabulous award-winning preserves under the name 'The Green Apron'. I make the preserves in small batches from Mom's original recipes, as well as others I've developed myself, and I use home-grown, wild and locally sourced produce when possible. We have won many national and international awards for the preserves and are listed in the Irish food guides.

Being both a gardener and a cook means that my life revolves around the growing and harvesting year. I look forward to January because it's Seville orange season and it's time to get marmalade-making. After the Sevilles come the blood oranges and other new-season citrus for even more marmalades and to brighten our end-of-winter cooking. Then I'm out in the garden in the spring watching the rhubarb slowly unfurl, and I'm greedily harvesting the stalks when they are still only finger-length because I can't wait for that first pie. My favourite food day of the year is when my first courgettes are finally ready – again, harvested ridiculously small, but they are so tender and delicious. (I always grow a few plants in the greenhouse just to get a super early crop.) Next comes the berry harvest with its abundance of strawberries, raspberries, blackcurrants and other soft fruit. So much fruit, so little time. Days of walking along rows of berries, picking, getting scratched, eating more berries than ever end up in the basket and then home to make cordials, summer jams, pies or just bowls of fruit and cream. And let us not forget that it's also time for figs, and the stone fruit such as cherries, nectarines, peaches and apricots to come into season. Ah, summer.

After the soft-fruit season, it's time for the first of the wild fruit to ripen. Who hasn't been tempted by the hedgerow of newly ripened juicy blackberries and improvised a berry-carrying receptacle from a hat or shirt? Every country walk slows down as we pick the hedges, and every hill walk involves a search for the elusive fraughan (the wild blueberry). I spend months out harvesting the hedgerows, using some fruit fresh (blackberry pie, anyone?) and storing the rest in the freezer until I get time to turn it into preserves.

Then the gardens and orchards fill with apples, pears and plums, and the hedges with haws, hips, sloes and more berries. Such a bounty. I greedily gather all that I can, and the kitchen is filled with bowls and baskets of fruit, which I turn into autumn chutneys, jellies and jams. The kitchen smells of nothing but vinegar, spices and fruit for weeks. There is an abundance of wild fruit available in late summer and autumn in the hedges, but often the blackberries are the only fruit we really notice and harvest. Let's change that and start picking the sloes for gin, the hips and haws for jelly, the elderberries for syrup and the damsons for jam. They are free, taste great and are full of nutrition. Pumpkins, grapes and kiwis finish off our garden season – the pumpkins used for jack-o'-lanterns and then turned into soups, cakes and pies. Finally we are on to the clementines and cranberries of Christmas and the mounds of dried fruit for our cakes, pies and mincemeat. And then it's time for the Seville oranges again.

In this book I share some of my recipes with you. Some I invented, some I adapted from old recipes, and some have been given to me. They are all based on fruit and are almost all seasonal (except the pineapple and banana ones – but they were too delicious to not include). We grow a lot of fruit, and, as our business is based on using fruit, we are very aware of the seasons and what fruit is available. Some of the recipes here are simple, and some are more complex, but all are well within the reach of an ordinary home cook. Most use fruit grown on trees or bushes that fruit every year, but we do use some fruits that grow annually and are usually used in savoury dishes, such as peas, courgettes, tomatoes and cucumbers. I've included some recipes for these in the book as they are so easily grown at home or found in your local market.

I hope I can encourage you to grow some of your own fruit. Our temperate climate means we can grow a wide range, many more than you'd think. Did you know kiwis grow very well outside here? I didn't until we started growing them, and now they are taking over. Whether it's a pot of strawberries outside the door or a big walled orchard, we can all make some space to grow. There's such a sense of satisfaction in sitting down to a tart or a pot of your own jam, made from fruit you grew yourself.

Year's Beginning

Seville orange marmalade

Seville oranges are only available in January. They are bitter, seed-filled oranges – not good for eating raw but they make the best marmalade. My preserving year starts the first week of January, when I get my Seville oranges. And I'm not the only one. Across the country, houses are filled with steam and the smell of orange peel, and kitchen tables are covered in bowls of chopped oranges and peel, bags of sugar and mismatched glass jars. Makes 4.5 kg (10 lbs).

1.35 kg (3 lb) Seville oranges

2 medium lemons

3.4 l (6 pints) water

2.7 kg (6 lb) sugar

1   Wash the Seville oranges and the lemons. Remove any blemishes from the skin and cut them into quarters.

2   Place in a food processor and process on high speed for 20 seconds. Then check to see if the peel is reduced to pieces about 6 mm (¼ inch) in size. Continue to process in 5-second bursts until it is. If you like bigger peel in your marmalade, don't process it for so long, and if you like very little peel, process it for longer. Don't worry about the seeds. When you add the sugar they usually all float up to the top of the pot and you can skim them off.

3   Put the processed oranges and lemons in a preserving pot with the water and cook on a high heat until the mixture begins to boil. Reduce the heat to medium and continue to cook until the peel is cooked and smooshes to tiny pieces between your fingers. This usually takes about an hour.

4   Add the sugar, stir well and bring the temperature up to full again. All of the seeds should float to the top so you can skim them off with a spoon. Cook on high heat until the marmalade reaches setting point (see p. 196). This can take anything from 20–40 minutes or even longer. Remove from the heat and skim off any remaining seeds or sugar foam.

5   Move the pot to a clear work surface. Pour into warm sterilised jars to within 6 mm (¼ inch) of the top, lid and seal.

TIP: Always wash citrus fruit very well as it may have been sprayed to prolong its shelf life. Try to use organic citrus fruit if possible. Give the fruit a good scrub with your vegetable brush under a running tap.

Marmalade tarts

We always seemed to have a stash of these in the cupboard when I was growing up. As you popped the lid of the tin, the delicious smell of orange and pastry wafted up, and you knew it was time for tea. If you use coarse marmalade, you will get delicious chewy orangey bits in the batter, but use whatever you have to hand. I make these in shallow bun tins: round-bottom ones are the best (muffin tins are too deep) and store them in an airtight container for up to a week. Makes 12.

SHORTCRUST PASTRY

110 g (4 oz) butter (chopped)

225 g (8 oz) plain flour

½ tsp salt

6 tbsp cold water

BATTER

75 g (2½ oz) plain flour

¼ tsp baking powder

60 g (2 oz) butter (chopped)

60 g (2 oz) sugar

1 large egg (beaten)

1 tbsp marmalade

1 Rub the butter into the flour until it resembles fine breadcrumbs and then mix in the salt. Add the cold water, a tablespoon at a time, mixing after each addition until the pastry holds together. You may not need to use it all. Knead it a few times until it is smooth and then cover it and put it in the fridge to rest for at least 30 minutes.

2 Preheat the oven to 200°C (400°F/Gas 6).

3 Roll out the pastry on a floured surface until it is about 3 mm (⅛ inch) thick (or thicker if it's very crumbly). Cut out circles slightly bigger than the size of the bun hole and put them into the tin.

4 Mix the flour, baking powder, butter, sugar and egg together until smooth. I do this in my food processor.

5 Fold in the marmalade.

6 Put 1 teaspoon of the batter into each pastry case.

7 Bake the tarts for 18–20 minutes until golden brown.

8 Remove the bun tin from the oven. Let the tarts cool in the tin for a few minutes and then carefully take them out and place them on a wire rack to finish cooling.

TIP: If you have leftover pastry, cut out more pastry circles and pop them in the freezer for the next time you are making tarts. Freeze flat on a baking tray and then transfer them into a freezer bag. Never waste pastry!

Marmalade granola

Granola tastes so much better than muesli and is almost as good for you. I use marmalade in mine instead of sugar, honey or golden syrup as I feel it gives more flavour and texture. My kids eat it with milk and chopped apple. I like chopped banana or strawberries and yogurt with mine, and I've seen people eat it with apple juice, so it's a great way of getting a bit of extra fresh fruit into your day. Makes about 2.5 kg (5 lb).

900 g (2 lb) porridge oats

200 g (7 oz) desiccated coconut

90 g (3 oz) flaked almonds

90 g (3 oz) sunflower seeds

90 g (3 oz) pumpkin seeds

3 tbsp linseeds

4 tbsp marmalade

3 tbsp sunflower oil

450 g (1 lb) dried apricots (chopped finely)

450 g (1 lb) raisins

1 tsp cinnamon

1 Preheat the oven to 160°C (325°F/Gas 2). Mix the oats, coconut, almonds, sunflower seeds, pumpkin seeds and linseeds together in a large bowl.

2 Put the marmalade into a small bowl and mash it with a fork until it is mushed into a paste. Mix through the oat mixture.

3 Drizzle the sunflower oil over the oat mixture and mix through. Spread it about an inch deep on a baking tray and put in the oven to bake.

4 Check it after 10 minutes and stir it around (the granola at the sides cooks much faster). Keep checking and stirring every 10 minutes until it's light golden brown. This should take about 40 minutes.

5 Remove the tray from the oven and pour the cooked oats back into the mixing bowl. Add the dried fruit and the cinnamon and mix through.

6 Let the granola cool completely, then place in an airtight container.

Variations
For this recipe I used raisins and apricots, but add any dried fruit you like: figs, prunes, bananas, etc. Likewise with the nuts and seeds.

Marmalade cocktail

We love experimenting with cocktails. (My daughter Bella is our cocktail queen.) Instead of buying all those expensive, coloured, fruity cocktail ingredients, we now use jam and marmalade for a burst of real fruit flavour, colour and sweetness. Makes one cocktail.

2 tsp marmalade

2–3 dashes of Angostura bitters

60 ml (2 fl. oz) whiskey

1 tbsp simple syrup

Ice cubes

Sparkling water

1 Muddle the marmalade, bitters and whiskey together until the marmalade starts to dissolve.

2 Add the simple syrup. (To make simple syrup, mix equal amounts of water and sugar and heat until the sugar dissolves. Allow to cool completely and keep in the fridge. Use within a few weeks.)

3 Drink neat over ice or add sparkling water to make a longer drink.

Growing citrus

When we went to Sorrento on honeymoon, I was amazed by the sight of all the lemon and orange trees growing outside, and not only growing outside but growing everywhere and on every and any bit of waste ground – like sycamores or ash here. While I technically knew that citrus trees grow outside in warm climes, the sight of them boggled my mind (boggled it!). We can grow citrus trees here, but they need to be in heated greenhouses or in orangeries. (Sunrooms are technically orangeries.) You can grow your citrus tree from seed, which is fun but will take many years to fruit and may not produce a decent crop of good fruit after all that effort – seedling trees often produce different fruit from the parents. So buy yourself a good variety from a specialist nursery and hopefully in a few years you'll be using your own lemons for lemon curd. I planted a handful of seeds from my Seville oranges this year. They germinated within a month, and I now have nine baby trees. I'll keep these in my heated greenhouse, and, even if I don't get a crop of marmalade oranges, I'll be rewarded with wonderful fragrant blooms and scented leaves.

Blood-orange marmalade

Blood oranges are usually only in the shops for a few weeks in February, so I try to make the most of them by using them in salads, cakes, marmalades and juices during that time. They are quite sweet, rather like a clementine, with bright red flesh and occasionally red peel. Makes 4.5 kg (10 lb).

4 lemons

3.4 l (6 pints) water

1 kg (2¼ lb) blood oranges

2.7 kg (6 lb) sugar

1 Wash the lemons, quarter them and then process into rice-sized pieces in a food processor. Place in a preserving pan with the water.

2 Wash and quarter the blood oranges and process into pea-sized pieces. Add to the preserving pan.

3 Cook the fruit mixture on a high heat until the peel softens and smooshes into small pieces between your fingers.

4 Add the sugar and cook until the marmalade reaches setting point (see p. 196). Then remove from the stove.

5 Pour into warm sterilised jars to within 6 mm (¼ inch) of the top, lid and seal.

Pirate marmalade (blood-orange and black rum marmalade)
One year, when pirate movies were all the rage, the kids all started talking like pirates any time they saw my regular blood-orange marmalade. So I decided to make a much more piratey version with black rum and allspice. Now we all have to restrain ourselves from talking like pirates when we sell it in the market. (Arrgghh, me hearties!) Follow the recipe for blood-orange marmalade, and, when it has reached setting point, remove it from the heat and add 1 teaspoon ground allspice and 60 ml (2 fl. oz) black Jamaica rum and stir through. Then jar, lid and seal as usual.

Oh my darlin' Clementine marmalade
Use the same recipe as for blood-orange marmalade, just replace the blood oranges with clementines. This is a light, sweet marmalade for those who don't like the bitterness of traditional marmalade. We also use satsumas, mandarins, clementines and mandoras – whatever sweet wee orange is in season.

Vin d'orange

In parts of southern France, almost every garden has a Seville orange tree – not for marmalade-making but for this delicious wine liqueur. My friend Nancy, a regular visitor to southern France, kindly shared this recipe with me. I happily sacrifice some of my precious marmalade oranges to make this delicious wine and think of sitting in the summer sun drinking the finished liqueur. It's bitter-sweet, rather like Pimm's, and is usually ready just as the weather gets nice enough for us to think about sitting outdoors. We drink it splashed into white wine or champagne or mixed with lemonade or ginger ale. My sister-in-law, Una, drinks it in her gin and tonics: equal amounts gin and vin d'orange over ice, topped up with tonic water. Nancy says to be sure to use a dry French rosé, not a sweet American one. She uses two 5-l plastic water bottles to hold her vin d'orange while it is steeping. Makes about 5 l (9 pints).

---

5 Seville oranges (washed and cut into eighths)

2 sweet oranges (washed and cut into eighths)

Peel of 1 lemon

4 l (7 pints) dry rosé wine

1 l (1¾ pints) vodka (unflavoured)

1 kg (2¼ lb) sugar

1 vanilla pod

1 clove

1 Mix all the ingredients together in a large (10-l) glass or plastic container and stir well.

2 Cover and leave in a cool, dark place for at least 4 weeks, stirring or shaking regularly.

3 Filter out the fruit and spices and discard.

4 Put the liqueur into bottles, seal and keep in a dark cupboard. It should keep for years.

Three-fruit marmalade

When you've eaten all your Seville orange marmalade and you're looking into a marmaladeless abyss, this mixture of grapefruit, sweet oranges and lemons is the one to make. The grapefruits add bitterness, the oranges add the orange flavour, and the lemons bind it all together and help it to set. We make this all through the year, and it's one of our best-selling preserves. For four-fruit marmalade, add a lime. Makes 4.5 kg (10 lb).

1 ruby grapefruit

2 medium sweet oranges

4 lemons

3.4 l (6 pints) water

2.7 kg (6 lb) sugar

1 Wash the grapefruit, oranges and lemons. Remove any blemishes from the skin and cut them into quarters. Place in the food processor and process on high speed until the peel is reduced to 6-mm (¼-inch) pieces. If you like bigger peel in your marmalade, don't process it for so long, and if you like very little peel, process it for longer.

2 Put the processed citrus in a preserving pot with the water, stir well and cook on a high heat, stirring occasionally, until the peel is cooked and smooshes to wee pieces between your fingers. This usually takes an hour.

3 Add the sugar, stir well and cook over a high heat, stirring occasionally, until the marmalade reaches setting point (see p. 196), then remove from the heat. Skim off any seeds and sugar foam.

4 Pour into warm sterilised jars to within 6 mm (¼ inch) of the top, lid and seal.

TIP: I use ruby grapefruit because it adds a great colour, but you can use regular yellow grapefruit.

Irish whiskey marmalade
Our Irish whiskey marmalade is very popular at the market, especially in colder weather – I guess whiskey for breakfast makes those cold dreary mornings that wee bit better. It also won a Bronze Blas na hÉireann Award in 2015. Prepare the three-fruit marmalade to setting point, then remove from the heat and stir in 60 ml (2 fl. oz) of good Irish whiskey and 1 teaspoon of ground mixed spice. Pour into jars, lid and seal.

Grapefruit and apple mint cookies

I love grapefruit. I eat it for breakfast, add it to salads, grill it covered with brown sugar and juice it. But when my daughters found a cookie recipe that combined grapefruit and apple mint, I was dubious. I didn't think grapefruit and apple mint were a good match. I was so wrong. Apple mint is a sweet, fruity variety that grows readily here (it's taking over my herb garden) and is available in most garden centres and markets. The original recipe made a very crumbly cookie, so my daughter Bella (our baking queen) experimented, adapting one of Mrs Beeton's. Keep in an airtight tin, and they should last for at least a week. Makes 3 dozen.

---

110 g (4 oz) butter

110 g (4 oz) sugar

1 egg

Zest of 1 medium grapefruit, finely grated

3 tsp finely chopped fresh apple mint

1 tsp baking powder

225 g (8 oz) plain flour

1 Preheat the oven to 160°C (325°F/Gas 3) and grease two or more large baking trays.

2 Beat the butter and sugar together until smooth.

3 Beat in the egg, grapefruit zest and chopped apple mint.

4 Add the baking powder and flour and mix well until you have a soft dough. (I do all this in the food processor.)

5 Using a teaspoonful of dough at a time, make about 3 dozen small balls. Place these on the baking trays and flatten slightly with a fork. The cookies will expand, so space them out well.

6 Bake for 15–20 minutes until golden brown, turning the tray halfway through cooking. Remove from the oven and leave to cool on the tray for a few minutes until they get hard enough to move. Then place them on a wire rack to finish cooling.

Lemon and coconut cake

This is one of the first cakes I taught my kids to bake, as it's simple, quick to make and delicious. It's one of my mom's recipes; she used to bake this cake to sell in the market. It keeps for up to 2 weeks in an airtight tin and freezes well. Makes either a small loaf (21×11×6 cm/8½×4½×2½ inches) or 12 individual buns.

CAKE

1 tsp grated lemon peel

170 g (6 oz) plain flour

1 tsp baking powder

110 g (4 oz) butter

110 g (4 oz) sugar

2 medium eggs

75 ml (2½ fl. oz) milk

60 g (2 oz) desiccated coconut

TOPPING

1 tbsp lemon juice

1 tbsp caster sugar

2 tbsp desiccated coconut

1 Preheat the oven to 160°C (325°F/Gas 3).

2 Place the lemon peel, flour, baking powder, butter, sugar, eggs and milk into a mixer and beat for about 2 minutes until smooth and glossy. Fold in the coconut.

3 Pour into parchment-lined tins, filling them only two-thirds full.

4 Bake for 25–35 minutes for small cakes or 50 minutes to an hour for larger cakes until they are a light golden brown and an inserted skewer comes out clean. Remove from the oven and let cool in the tin. When cool, remove from the tin and place right side up on a wire rack.

5 For the topping, mix the lemon juice and the caster sugar together. Brush this mixture over the top of the cooled cake. Sprinkle the coconut all across the top. Leave to sit for a few minutes, then it's ready to eat.

Lemon curd

I adore lemon curd, but it always seemed too much trouble to make ... until one of my fellow ICA ladies, Anne, told me she makes hers in the microwave. Armed with this new information, I went back through my pile of preserving books and invented this. I use a large grater (like a cheese grater) as I love the texture of the zest, but you can grate it more finely. Don't grate the white pith as it can make the curd bitter. The curd will keep for 3 weeks in the fridge, if it lasts that long. This recipe can be used for any citrus: blood orange, clementine, grapefruit, lime, etc., and makes approximately 400 g (14 oz).

---

3 large lemons

110 g (4 oz) butter

2 large eggs

225 g (8 oz) sugar

TIP: To get the most juice from your lemon, roll it on a hard surface, applying lots of pressure with your hand. It will start to break up the internal structure of the fruit and make it easier to juice.

1 Wash the lemons and carefully grate the zest off all three. Juice two of the lemons and measure the juice. You want about 5 tablespoons. If you don't have enough, juice the last one.

2 Put the butter in a small bowl and microwave on medium heat for about a minute until soft and starting to melt. Remove from the microwave, stir to distribute the heat evenly and then set aside.

3 Whisk the eggs and sugar together in a large bowl until just combined. Add the lemon zest and juice and stir through.

4 Add the softened butter and whisk the whole lot together until combined.

5 Place the bowl of curd mixture into the microwave and cook on medium heat for 1 minute. Take it out, give it a quick whisk, and put it back in for another minute. Cook it in 1-minute bursts on medium heat until thick enough to coat the back of a spoon. (It takes me about 5 minutes.) Beware of overcooking: it thickens as it cools.

6 Taste the curd. If it needs more lemon, add some more juice, a teaspoon at a time, until you are happy with the flavour, and then microwave it for another minute to incorporate the newly added juice.

7 Now it's ready to eat, so pour it into warm sterilised jars, lid and seal.

Serving suggestions
Slather the warm curd onto hot toast. Make lemon-curd tarts using my jam-tart recipe (see p. 74). Swirl it through yogurt for breakfast and use it as a dessert topping. Lash it on scones (with cream of course) and layer it through cakes.

Mojito marmalade

This marmalade tastes like a summer sunshine cocktail in a jar. I use a mix of limes and lemons as I find lime-only marmalade too strong – this recipe has the perfect balance of flavours for me. Makes 4.5 kg (10 lb).

5 limes

4 medium lemons

3.4 l (6 pints) water

2.7 kg (6 lb) sugar

2 handfuls/packets of fresh mint

1 Wash the limes, cut into quarters and then whizz in a food processor until they are in rice-sized pieces.

2 Wash the lemons, cut into quarters and add these to the processor. Whizz until the lemons are also rice-sized. The lime pieces are so hard they won't reduce much in size while the lemons are being cut down.

3 Put the fruit into a preserving pan with the water. Cook on a high heat, stirring occasionally, until the pieces of peel smoosh into tiny pieces between your fingers.

4 Add the sugar and stir well.

5 Roll a rolling pin across the top of the mint to bruise it slightly and then wrap it in a piece of cheesecloth. Tie the cloth tight, so the mint can't escape, and add this to the pot.

6 Cook over high heat (occasionally pushing the bag of mint against the side of the pot to release more flavour), stirring occasionally, until the marmalade reaches setting point (see p. 196). Skim off any seeds that float to the top and remove the mint.

7 Pour into warm sterilised jars to within 6 mm (¼ inch) of the top of the jar, lid and seal.

Mojito marmalade mojito
Try making a real mojito from the marmalade. Stir a tablespoonful of marmalade into a shot of white rum and then top up with soda water or white lemonade. Garnish with lime and mint.

Variation
Make a lemon and lime marmalade by leaving out the mint.

Beef with orange

My family calls this an 'orange pot' recipe after my mom's big orange Le Creuset which she uses for all her slow-cooked casseroles and savoury stews. When it appears at the table you know dinner is going to be rich and delicious before the lid is even raised. The recipe is a tweaked version of Mom's (mainly I added booze) and is the perfect winter warmer. It's an excellent recipe for visitors as you can make it days before and reheat. Serve in a bowl with mashed potato or buttered noodles. Serves 4.

2 tbsp olive oil

3 small onions (thinly sliced)

1 streaky smoked bacon rasher (rind removed and finely chopped)

680 g (1½ lb) rib steak beef (cubed)

2 cloves of garlic (peeled and finely chopped)

1 tbsp plain flour

600 ml (1 pint) beef stock

1 small bay leaf

1 tsp whole black peppercorns

150 ml (¼ pint) red wine (or stout)

1 medium orange

1 tbsp tomato purée

½ tsp chopped fresh thyme

1 Heat the olive oil in an ovenproof pot and fry the onions, bacon and beef over a medium heat for a few minutes until the meat is brown and the onions start to turn golden.

2 Add the garlic and cook for about 1 minute.

3 Now add the flour and stir it through everything. It will get a bit dry and sandy.

4 Pour the beef stock into the pot and stir everything well.

5 Add the bay leaf, peppercorns, wine, the zest and juice of the orange, tomato purée and thyme and mix well.

6 Put a lid on the pot and pop into the oven for 1½ hours at 160°C (325°F/Gas 3) or until the beef is tender.

7 Taste the casserole, season and serve.

Orange and sweet potato soup

I'm a big fan of sweet potatoes. They're full of nutrients and beta-carotene, and they last for ages in your larder. This is an excellent rich and creamy winter soup, and the sharpness of the orange balances the sweetness of the potato. You can use any sweet orange for this recipe: blood orange, Valencia orange or clementine. Serve with a dollop of sour cream or yogurt. Serves 4–5.

3 tbsp olive oil or butter

1 large onion (diced)

2 cloves of garlic (chopped)

1 large sweet potato (about 680 g or 1½ lb, peeled and diced)

1 l (1¾ pint) vegetable or chicken stock

1 medium orange

Salt and pepper

1 Heat the olive oil or butter in a large saucepan over a medium heat. Add the onion and cook it until the edges go dark brown. You want the flavour that comes from that brown!

2 Add the garlic and sweet potato and stir through.

3 Then add the stock and cook, covered, for about 15 minutes over a medium heat until the sweet potato can be mashed against the side of the pan with a fork.

4 Take the pan off the heat and blend the soup to a smooth creamy consistency using a blender or food processor. Put the blended soup back into the saucepan.

5 Add the juice and zest of the orange and stir through. Heat the soup gently until steaming. Don't let it boil as that will dull the fresh orange flavour. Add salt and pepper to taste and then serve.

Variations

To make a heartier soup, add a cup of red lentils, increase the volume of the stock to 1.5 litres (2½ pints) and extend the cooking time to about 30 minutes. If you like a bit of heat, add a pinch of flaked chilli to the soup as it's cooking. Or substitute a can of coconut milk for some of the stock and add grated fresh ginger, chopped chilli and fresh coriander at the end of cooking.

Rhubarb and coriander meringue pie

For this recipe, I took Mom's rhubarb meringue pie recipe and tweaked it. Coriander adds an earthy depth and offsets the rhubarb's sharpness. I usually use green rhubarb as that is what we grow. You can use red food colouring to make the rhubarb mixture pink, but I don't bother. Makes a 23-cm (9-inch) pie.

SHORTCRUST PASTRY

110 g (4 oz) butter (chopped)

225 g (8 oz) plain flour

½ tsp salt

6 tbsp cold water

PIE FILLING

450 g (1 lb) rhubarb (cut into 2.5-cm/1-inch pieces)

2 tbsp water

¼ tsp ground coriander

75 g (2½ oz) sugar

2 tbsp cornflour

2 egg yolks (lightly beaten)

MERINGUE TOPPING

2 egg whites

110 g (4 oz) caster sugar

1 Rub the butter into the flour until it resembles fine breadcrumbs and then mix in the salt. Add the water, a tablespoon at a time, mixing after each addition, until the pastry holds together. You may not need to use it all. Knead it a few times until it is smooth and then cover and put in the fridge to rest for at least 30 minutes.

2 Preheat the oven to 190°C (375°F/Gas 5).

3 Line a 23-cm (9-inch) pie dish with the pastry and crimp the edges. Prick holes in the bottom and bake for 20 minutes. Remove from the oven and leave to cool. Turn the oven up to 200°C (400°F/Gas 6).

4 In a saucepan over a low heat, gently poach the rhubarb in the water, coriander and sugar until it starts to soften. You want to keep the pieces of rhubarb as whole as possible. Taste it and adjust the spice or sugar if you need to.

5 Carefully pour the cooked rhubarb into a sieve and drain the juice. Pour the juice back into the pan, add the cornflour, mix well, and cook, stirring continuously over a medium heat, until it thickens. It should be the consistency of thick custard.

6 Put the pieces of rhubarb back into the pan of juice and mix through carefully. Then fold in the egg yolks. Pour this mixture into the pie crust.

7 Whisk the egg whites until they form stiff peaks and then slowly whisk in the sugar, a teaspoonful at a time. (Make sure the sugar is well mixed.)

8 Spoon the meringue mixture over the fruit. For best results, the fruit filling should be warm to help the meringue stick to the fruit. If the fruit has cooled, pop the pie into the oven for a few minutes until the filling just starts to steam.

9 Bake the pie for a few minutes until the meringue is set and golden brown.

Pie 101

I prefer deep American-style pies to the Irish fruit tart as I want a high fruit to pastry ratio. The main problem with making a deep-dish pie with raw fruit is that is that the pastry often cooks well before the filling and so you either have slightly uncooked insides or rock-hard or burnt outsides. The second problem is that the filling is often too runny, and you end up with sloppy berriness all over your plate instead of inside your pie. The answer to both these problems is to cook the filling first, and I now do this for most of my pies. I cook the fruit, sweeten and flavour it and then thicken it, usually with cornflour.

I like cornflour as my thickener because it gives a consistent result. I have used tapioca, regular flour and arrowroot, but I still go back to cornflour. If your fruit is very juicy, add more cornflour. The filling should be the consistency of thick porridge or custard. It will thicken more once it's cool, but you need it fairly thick in the pot. Frozen berries will need a bit more thickener, and, if you add more sugar to the recipe, add a bit more thickener too.

A very basic American pie filling recipe is 4–6 cups of fruit, a half to 1 cup of sugar, 3 tablespoons of cornflour, a half teaspoon of flavouring and a few tablespoons of water. (Use a teacup if you don't have an American cup measure.) This makes enough for a 23-cm (9-inch) deep pie. Soften the fruit in water, then add the sugar, flavouring and cornflour and cook until thickened. Experiment. Add weird things like chocolate and nuts. (We developed a raspberry chocolate walnut pie this way.)

I use a butter shortcrust pastry for all my pies. I don't sweeten it as the filling is usually sweet enough. The shortcrust will last for about 3 days in the fridge and up to 3 months in the freezer. If you can't be bothered making pastry, just buy it in a supermarket. If you want to be very sure that your pie has a nice crisp bottom, prebake your bottom crust at 190°C (375°F/Gas 5) for 20 minutes or so, then add the filling and topping and rebake. You may need to cover the edges of the crust with tin foil to stop them burning.

I use cinnamon in a lot of my fruit pies as it goes well with apples, peaches and plums. Add lemon juice or zest (or both) to berry fillings to sharpen up the flavour. Add almond essence to cherry and peach. Use white sugar for sweetening the delicate flavoured summer berries as brown might affect the colour and taste. Other fruit, such as apples and peaches, cry out for brown sugar.

Once you've filled your pie, you need to decide how to cover it: full pie crust, lattice, streusel or meringue. It depends on the fruit and on what you are after. You can also leave it bare. If you want a pie that holds together well and is transportable, use a full pie-crust lid. If you're like me and you love being able to see the bubbly fruit, use a lattice. I love lattice crusts so much I bought a lattice roller so I could make them quickly and easily. Streusel is a great, quick topping. It's basically a crumble, and I use it on apple, peach, plum and rhubarb pies. Mix 110 g (4 oz) melted butter, 90 g (3 oz) brown sugar, 140 g (5 oz) flour and a pinch of salt together and sprinkle across the fruit filling. Meringue makes a good topping for acidic fruit pies such as rhubarb, but make sure the fruit filling is warm when you put the meringue on to get it to stick to the fruit. You don't want your meringue to slide off!

Rhubarb and orange coffee cake

There's no coffee in this cake. It's meant to be eaten *with* coffee, either as breakfast or for elevenses. I found the recipe in one of Grandma's books and added the orange peel and zest for an extra zing. Coffee cakes are best eaten on the day they are made, but if you don't manage to finish it, wrap it up and pop it in the freezer for another day. Serve with cream or yogurt or spread with butter. Makes a 33×23×5-cm (13×9×2-inch) cake – that's 12 large servings.

CAKE

110 g (4 oz) butter (chopped)

280 g (10 oz) sugar

250 ml (9 fl. oz) buttermilk or sour milk

1 egg

1 tsp vanilla essence

1 tsp baking powder

½ tsp salt

310 g (11 oz) plain flour

1 medium orange (juice and zest)

400 g (14 oz) rhubarb chopped into 1-cm (½-inch) pieces

TOPPING

170 g (6 oz) brown sugar

60 g (2 oz) chopped walnuts

1 Preheat the oven to 180°C (350°F/Gas 4) and grease a 33×23×5-cm (13×9×2-inch) cake pan.

2 Put all of the cake ingredients except the rhubarb into a food processor and mix at medium speed for 2 or 3 minutes until smooth.

3 Add the rhubarb pieces to the batter, mix gently and pour into the greased cake pan.

4 For the topping, mix together the sugar and the nuts. Sprinkle on top of the cake batter.

5 Bake for 45 minutes until golden on top and cooked through. Take out of the oven and leave to cool for 5 minutes or so before serving.

Variation

If I'm making this cake for a bake sale or coffee morning, I will spread the batter into a parchment-lined baking tray (39×27 cm/15×11 inch) instead of a cake pan and cook it for a little less time – about 30 minutes. This makes it much easier to portion out neatly.

Rhubarb and ginger jam

I love rhubarb jam, but it's a pain to make. The rhubarb needs a lot of lemon to get it to set and then it sticks to the bottom of the pot as it thickens and tries to burn so it needs careful watching. It also starts to spit jam out of the pot and all over the stove and you. Is it worth it? Yes! It's delicious, but be greedy and keep it all for yourself. Makes 4.5 kg (10 lb).

2.7 kg (6 lb) rhubarb (cut into 2.5-cm or 1-inch slices)

900 ml (1½ pint) water

2.5 cm (1 inch) fresh ginger (grated)

Juice of 4 lemons

2.7 kg (6 lb) sugar

1 tsp ground ginger

1 Put the rhubarb, water, ginger and lemon juice in a preserving pan and cook on a medium heat, stirring occasionally, for about 30 minutes until the rhubarb pieces start to disintegrate.

2 Add the sugar, stir in well, and cook the jam over a high heat until setting point is reached (about 30–40 minutes; see p. 195). The jam will tend to stick to the bottom as it approaches the setting point so watch it carefully and stir it every few minutes. You may want to wear an oven glove as it will spit all over your hand.

3 Remove the pot from the stove. Add the ground ginger and mix through. Taste the jam and add more ground ginger if you like a stronger flavour.

4 Pour into warm sterilised jars to within 6 mm (¼ inch) of the top, lid and seal.

Variations
You can leave out the ginger or add ground coriander or coriander seeds instead.

Growing rhubarb

While rhubarb is not technically a fruit, I've included it because we use it as such. I consider it to be one of the easiest plants to grow. Just plant it in a sunny position in a weed-free, well-drained, moist soil (with lots of well-rotted manure dug in) and keep it reasonably weed-free until it is established. After that, its own leaves shade out any weeds. (I love a no-weeding plant.) It can be grown from seed or from pieces taken from an existing plant (crowns). A well-situated rhubarb patch full of happy plants can continue to produce a good crop for 20 years or more. Rhubarb plants increase in size every year so growers are often quite happy to share crowns from their plants in spring. My friend Nell gave me some of hers from a variety her parents planted back in the early 1900s. It cropped from spring through summer and was renowned through the county for its flavour. She had the best rhubarb tarts.

Russian rhubarb relish

This is the first of the new growing season's savoury preserves – thick and sweet and sour and spiced. Exactly what you want on cheese or meat, or on pudding, black or white. You'll eat it on everything. Ginger and coriander are the classic rhubarb spices, and they are perfect in this. The onions lend a tangy sweetness. It will keep for 3 weeks in the fridge or for around 3 months in sterilised jars. Makes 680 g (1½ lb).

250 g (9 oz) rhubarb (chopped into 1-cm/½-inch pieces)

250 g (9 oz) onion (thinly sliced)

350 g (12 oz) brown sugar

250 ml (9 fl. oz) vinegar

1½ tsp salt

½ tsp finely chopped fresh ginger

½ tsp coriander seeds (cracked)

¼ tsp ground allspice

Pinch of cayenne pepper

Pinch of black pepper

1 Put all the ingredients into a heavy-bottomed saucepan.

2 Cook over a medium heat for about 40 minutes, stirring occasionally, until the relish has darkened, is the consistency of thick jam and starts to stick to the bottom of the pot.

3 Either pour into warm sterilised jars, lid and seal or just pop in a bowl and keep it in the fridge. It will last for at least 3 weeks, if you don't eat it all first!

Spring orange smoothie

Here's a simple, fast recipe based on the Orange Julius, the drink of choice in every American mall. The oranges thicken the milk slightly so it has the consistency of a milkshake, and it tastes like an orange split ice pop. Yum! If you like your smoothie extra cold you can use frozen (peeled) oranges. Serves 2.

---

4 sweet oranges

600 ml (1 pint) milk (or thin natural yogurt)

1 tsp vanilla extract

Honey (optional)

1 Peel the oranges and divide them into quarters.

2 Blend them with the milk or yogurt and the vanilla extract until smooth.

3 Taste and add some honey for sweetness if required.

Smoothies 101

Any fruit normally eaten raw can be used in a smoothie, but mix blander fruit with more intensely flavoured ones. A plain banana smoothie is just sweet mush, but a banana and orange smoothie is delicious and zingy. I regularly add leafy greens, such as spinach and kale, to my smoothies. I prefer to use 1 part green to 3 parts fruit. I don't want my smoothie to taste too vegetabley. I often add chopped carrots or chopped beetroot: they add colour, nutrition and sweetness. Cut hard fruit, such as apple, into smaller pieces than soft fruit, such as banana. If you normally don't eat the peel (pineapple, citrus, mango, kiwi, passion fruit), then remove it first. The same goes for the seeds. Make up packs of fruit and have them in the freezer, ready to use.

I add fresh juice (usually orange or apple) rather than carton juice because it's more nutritious, but use what you have. I often use cooled tea. Well-flavoured herbal teas can add a great taste, and green tea gives that caffeine boost. I don't add ice cubes that might dilute the other ingredients – also, I don't want my smoothie teeth-achingly cold. If you like a cold smoothie, keep frozen fruit and frozen cubes of juice on hand.

Yogurt makes a more filling smoothie – and probiotic yogurt adds wonderful lactobacilli. Your insides will thank you. Milk adds calcium and makes the smoothie taste more like a delicious milkshake. Soy and nut milks are not just for the lactose intolerant: they can add a wonderful extra layer of flavour. Coconut water is delicious and nutritious. Kefir and kombucha both add probiotics and nutrients, but they can be quite strong-flavoured, so use carefully.

Use whatever you like best as a sweetener: honey, jam, agave syrup, maple syrup, dates, etc. Dates are especially good in green smoothies as they mask strong vegetable flavours. Vanilla adds sweetness and depth. Cinnamon also adds sweetness, meaning that less actual sweetener is needed. Fresh ginger adds a spicy kick and helps digestion. Peanut butter and other nut butters add protein, healthy fats and extra flavour. Or you might like to add cold-pressed oils such as flax seed. I sometimes add spirulina or other nutritional supplements for an added boost. I usually drink smoothies immediately, but they keep in the fridge for a few hours.

And the Living Is Easy

Strawberry glaze pie

I remember making this as a child: a very simple pie of fresh delicious strawberries set in their own thickened juice. It is best eaten on the day it's made, served with lashings of fresh whipped cream. Makes a 23-cm (9-inch) pie.

SHORTCRUST PASTRY

110 g (4 oz) butter (chopped)

225 g (8 oz) plain flour

½ tsp salt

6 tbsp cold water

PIE FILLING

680 g (1½ lb) strawberries (washed, hulled and sliced)

250 ml (9 fl. oz) water

140 g (5 oz) sugar

3 tbsp cornflour

TIP: Always wash your strawberries before you remove the hulls. This prevents water getting inside the berries during washing and stops them tasting watery.

1 Rub the butter into the flour until it resembles fine breadcrumbs and then mix in the salt. Add the water, a tablespoon at a time, mixing after each addition, until the pastry holds together. You may not need to use it all. Knead it a few times until it is smooth and then cover it and put in the fridge to rest for at least 30 minutes.

2 Preheat the oven to 190°C (375°F/Gas 5). Line a 23-cm (9-inch) pie dish with the pastry and crimp the edges. Prick holes in the bottom and bake for 20 minutes until golden. Remove from oven and leave to cool.

3 In a medium-size pot over a medium low heat, cook up 170 g (6 oz) of the strawberries with the water for about 2 minutes until soft. Stir to stop them sticking to the bottom. Mash the cooked strawberries with a potato masher and then push them through a sieve to make a purée.

4 Return the purée to the pot and add the sugar and the cornflour. Cook this mixture over a medium heat, stirring constantly, until it is thick and bubbly – about 3 minutes. It should be the consistency of thick custard. Remove from the heat.

5 Layer half of the remaining strawberries on the bottom of the pie crust and pour half of the thickened purée across the top. Put the other half of the strawberries on top of this and cover with the remainder of the purée.

6 Put into the fridge to chill for at least an hour.

Variation
There's an even simpler version of this pie. Instead of making a thickened syrup to cover the fresh berries, make a pint of packet strawberry jelly, pour that over the fruit and leave to set.

Growing 101

The most important part of growing your own fruit is deciding what you want to grow. Get a good fruit-growing book, such as *The New Fruit Expert* by D. G. Hessayon. (That's the one I use.) Select fruit you actually like. There's no point growing wonderful juicy pears if you can't stand the texture of pear. Research which varieties you want and how large you want the trees to grow. Do you want strawberries all year or just one season? Do you want dwarf apple trees or ones that are big enough to climb and hang a swing on? Don't pick plants that grow well in warm areas when you live on a cold north-facing hill unless you plan to grow them under cover. Talk to local fruit-growers and gardeners to see what grows well in your area. Buy good quality virus-free plants and trees from a fruit nursery. You are going to spend a lot of money putting in your fruit so make sure they are of decent quality. If someone wants to give you some of their plants, make sure they are very healthy – they could bring disease into your garden. Tempting and all as it is to buy those cheap trees and bushes in the supermarkets, think very carefully. If you have limited space, pick a tree or bush exactly suited to your needs and growing conditions, pay the extra money and get it from a nursery. If you have lots of space, knock yourself out and plant whatever you like – provided the plants are disease-free. Fruit bushes and trees prefer well-drained, moist, fertile soil, and most prefer sunlight. Keep the plants and trees well mulched and feed them in the spring. A healthy, happy plant is more resistant to disease and pests – and crops better too.

Strawberry spinach salad

This is our first salad of the berry season. We make it with strawberries and as the season progresses move on to raspberries, loganberries, blueberries and blackberries. If you don't have baby spinach, just remove the stems on the bigger leaves and tear them into small pieces. Makes enough for 4 small side salads or 1 salad for a greedy luncher.

SALAD

170 g (6 oz) strawberries (quartered)

1 bag (or a large bunch) baby spinach leaves

1 shallot (sliced very thin)

60 g (2 oz) walnuts or pecans (freshly toasted)

60 g (2 oz) goat's cheese or blue cheese (crumbled)

VINAIGRETTE

2 tbsp balsamic vinegar (or sherry vinegar)

1 tsp Dijon mustard

2 tbsp olive oil

Salt and pepper

1 Mix the salad ingredients together.

2 Whisk the vinegar, mustard and olive oil. Add salt and pepper to taste.

3 Toss the salad with the vinaigrette.

Growing strawberries

Grow as many strawberry plants as you can. Any berries you don't eat fresh can be frozen for later. You don't need a lot of space to grow them – they can be grown in window boxes, containers, hanging baskets or just planted in the garden. My favourite way is to plant up an 8×4-foot bed with twenty-four strawberry plants, a foot apart and a foot from the side of the bed. Then let them go mad. Strawberry plants send out runners with tiny plants strung along them. Each of those wee plants will root and grow. (They can be removed and planted elsewhere if you have too many.) By next year, the bed will be producing about a punnet of fruit per day during the fruiting season. That's a lot of berries. Choose a range of strawberry varieties that fruit across the season and you could be eating strawberries from May to the end of autumn.

Salads 101

The secret to the perfect salad is to have a variety of textures, shapes and flavours. Salads are not just fresh vegetables and fruit. I often cook up a batch of mixed grains – whole wheat, oats, brown rice and barley – and have a bowl of that stashed in the fridge to add to salads. I always cook more beans or chickpeas than I need so I have extra in the fridge, ditto with pasta, couscous, quinoa and bulgar. I don't use all of the elements listed below in every salad, but I do try to use at least five.

Greens (lettuce, spinach, chard, mixed leaves, kale, etc.)

Small fruit that pop in your mouth releasing juice: fresh currants, blueberries, pomegranate seeds, grapes

Savoury vegetable crunch: celery, grated carrot, raw beans, peas, broccoli, cauliflower, sprouted seeds

Soft and velvety fruit: raspberries, strawberries, avocados, bananas, peaches, apricots, nectarines, figs

Sweet (and a bit sour) crunch: apple, pear, kiwi, cherry tomatoes, roasted beetroot

Sprinkles: nuts and toasted seeds

Citrus: lime or lemon juice, orange or grapefruit pieces

Intense bursts of flavour: capers, olives, sundried tomato, marinated mushrooms, chopped shallots or scallions, pickles or chutneys

Edible flowers: nasturtiums, dandelions, calendula

Herbs: chopped basil, marjoram, oregano, tarragon, mint, chives

Protein: cheese, eggs, cold meats (chicken, beef, pork, chorizo, salami, sausages)

Dressing: olive oil and balsamic vinaigrette, Caesar dressing, mayonnaise, yogurt, Dijon mustard, white or red wine vinegar, or the fruity vinegar you made yourself

Carbohydrate: whole wheat, oats, brown rice, barley, beans, chickpeas, pasta, couscous, quinoa, bulgar

Lots of sea salt and black pepper

Layer up your salad: heavy ingredients on the bottom and lightest on the top. Season and dress each layer as you go. Think of the times you've got plain, boring, tasteless lettuce in a salad because the dressing didn't make it through to the bottom of the salad bowl. Don't let it happen again.

Strawberry butter

Simple though this recipe may be, it's surprisingly delicious. We use strawberry butter on scones, pancakes, toast and anything that can carry it to our mouths, for it is exceedingly good. If you use soft butter, the mixture looks curdled (it tastes great but just doesn't look right), so be sure to use cold butter. Makes about 400 g (14 oz).

225 g (8 oz) cold butter

1 tbsp icing sugar

170 g (6 oz) firm ripe strawberries (halved)

1 In a food processor, whizz the butter and icing sugar together until well combined.

2 Add half the strawberries and whizz until they disappear into the butter.

3 Now add the other half and pulse a few times until the berries are mixed through but you can still see little pieces. It should look a bit like a good ripple ice cream. Taste it and add more sugar or strawberries if the flavour isn't strong enough.

4 Put into dishes to keep in the fridge. It lasts for at least a week.

Variations
This recipe will also work with raspberries, blueberries or blackberries. Add a few strands of lemon zest to bring out their flavour.

Busy-day cake

Sometimes you just need cake, and you need it now. This is how I deal with these cake emergencies. It's fast, simple and doesn't need any icing to make it taste good. We cover it in berries and eat it throughout the summer. I made it all the time when I was in college, and it's one of the first cakes the kids learned to make by themselves. Makes a 20-cm (8-inch) cake.

CAKE

170 g (6 oz) plain flour

140 g (5 oz) sugar

2 tsp baking powder

160 ml (5½ fl. oz) milk

3 tbsp sunflower oil

1 egg

1¼ tsp vanilla essence

¼ tsp salt

TOPPING

250 g (9 oz) strawberries (washed and hulled)

1 tbsp sugar

1 Preheat the oven to 180°C (350°F/Gas 4). Grease a 20-cm (8-inch) cake pan.

2 Put all the ingredients into a mixing bowl and beat them together with a wooden spoon until you have a smooth batter.

3 Pour the batter into the cake pan and bake for 25 minutes or until golden brown. Leave to cool in the pan.

4 Thickly slice the strawberries and sprinkle with the sugar. Leave to sit for half an hour or until the juice starts to run from the berries.

5 Remove the cooled cake from the pan. I like to trim the edges so I can see the berry juice soaking through, but it's not necessary. Poke a few holes in the top of the cake for the juice to get in.

6 Carefully pour the juicy berries over the top of the cake. Serve with whipped cream and eat immediately.

Variations
You can replace the strawberries with raspberries or other berries or try lightly caramelised sliced peaches or nectarines. Sometimes I put lemon zest in the batter and then drizzle a lemon syrup on the finished cake. Add chocolate chips to the batter and then drizzle the cake with melted chocolate. You could also just ice it with butter-cream icing.

Strawberry jam

When I was about thirteen, I had five alpine strawberry plants. The berries were tiny, and I only got about a tablespoon of fruit from them every day. One day, I noticed my strawberries disappearing from the plants. I figured it was one of the sisters, or the dog. So I came up with a plan to stop the strawberry pilferage. I took a fresh chilli, cut it in half and wiped chilli juice all over the ripening fruit. Next morning there were terrible yells from the garden. (They were very hot chillies.) It wasn't my sisters, it was Dad! I got into some trouble for it, but my strawberries were safe after that. Nobody wanted to risk booby-trapped berries. Strawberry jam is still one of my favourites, and here is how we make ours. Makes about 3.5 kg (7½ lb).

---

2 kg (4½ lb) strawberries (hulled and halved if big)

Juice of 3 large lemons

150 ml (¼ pint) water

2 kg (4½ lb) sugar

1 Put the strawberries, lemon juice and the water into a preserving pot and cook over a low heat until the juice starts to run from the berries and they begin to soften. Remove the pot from the heat and put it onto a sturdy work surface.

2 Take a potato masher and squash the strawberries in the pot. You don't want them completely puréed, but you do want them broken up. Give it about six mashes.

3 Put the pot back onto the stove and continue to cook the fruit over a low heat until the strawberries are completely soft and the juice starts to darken in colour.

4 Add the sugar, stir in well, and cook on a high heat, stirring occasionally, until the jam reaches setting point (see p. 195). You want it to be barely set, because if you cook it for too long some of the flavour will be lost.

5 Pour into warm sterilised jars to within 6 mm (¼ inch) of the top, lid and seal.

Strawberry and rhubarb jam
Replace half the strawberries in this recipe with rhubarb. Cook the rhubarb in the water over a low heat until it starts to soften, then add the strawberries and lemon juice and cook until the strawberries are also soft. Then add the sugar and proceed as above.

Gooseberry or blackcurrant jam

Blackcurrants and gooseberries are both high in pectin and don't need separate setting agents. We add quite a bit of water so the individual berries are suspended in jelly in the pot. Many people don't add enough water or cook the berries for long enough and then the jam has a very chewy, dense texture. Use cooking gooseberries, not sweet dessert gooseberries. Makes 4.5 kg (10 lb).

1.8 kg (4 lb) gooseberries

1.8 litres (3 pints) water

2.7 kg (6 lb) sugar

1 Put the berries and water into a preserving pan and cook over a medium heat until the berries pop and the skin of one smooshes into tiny pieces between your fingers.

2 Add the sugar and stir through. Cook over a high heat, stirring occasionally, for about 25 minutes until it reaches setting point (see p. 195).

3 Pour into warm sterilised jars to within 6 mm (¼ inch) of the top, lid and seal.

Variation

Use jostaberries or any other gooseberry–blackcurrant hybrid.

TIP: Gooseberries and currants must be topped and tailed before they are used in cooking. This means removing the tiny remains of the flower blossoms still on the berry and the stem from the bottom.

Growing blackcurrants

Grow blackcurrants in good soil in full sun. A full-grown currant bush, given plenty of room, can grow 5 feet high and have a 5-foot spread, but I plant them in rows about 2 feet apart and use them as windbreak hedges in the garden. The hedge bushes are not as productive as individual bushes, but it saves space and gives shelter. To grow new bushes yourself, in winter, take 12-inch cuttings from this year's wood (that's the shiny straight silver-stemmed bits at the end of the branches). Cut the tips off the cuttings, and plant them 8 inches deep in a well-drained area of the garden. Leave the cuttings there until the following winter, when they should be well rooted, then move them to their permanent growing position.

Raspberry jam

This is a very good recipe. (I can't take credit; it's Mom's, and the technique is hers too.) It's our best-selling jam, and we won our first Blas na hÉireann award for it in 2010. The secret is to not overcook your jam. We cook ours until it is just barely setting. It's very sloppy, but the flavours haven't all been cooked off. Eat it within a few weeks – the longer it sits in the jar, the more the delicate fruit flavours break down and you are left with a vaguely fruity, sugary spread instead of the jar of summer you wanted. Makes 3.4 kg (7½ lb).

---

2 kg (4½ lb) raspberries

Juice of 2 lemons

2 kg (4½ lb) sugar

1 Place the raspberries and the lemon juice in a preserving pan and cook over a low heat, stirring occasionally, until the raspberries start to disintegrate and the juice begins to darken. This can take up to an hour.

2 Add the sugar, stir well and cook the jam over a high heat for about 10 minutes or until it just reaches setting point (see p. 195).

3 Pour into warm sterilised jars to within 6 mm (¼ inch) of the top, lid and seal.

Variation
Use this recipe for loganberries and tayberries.

TIP: Freeze some of your raspberries to make fresh jam through the year.

Growing raspberries

Raspberries are very easy to grow: put them in reasonable soil in a sunny area and watch them take off – and I mean take off: raspberry canes spread everywhere. Once you plant raspberries in the garden, you will have them for ever. Plant the canes in rows and mow between the lines to cut down the new baby canes – otherwise you'll have a raspberry jungle. Plant both summer and autumn fruiting varieties and you could be picking from early July to November. Propagate summer raspberries by digging up some of the extra canes that the plant has produced and replanting them. Cut newly planted canes back to 6 inches to allow the roots to get strong. Do this in late autumn.

Raspberry jam cocktail

This is a great summery cocktail that showcases your wonderful fresh raspberry jam. I don't strain my cocktails as I quite like the bits of fruit in them, but if you prefer a clearer drink, do strain it. I usually add sparkling water to make mine a longer drink. Makes one cocktail.

1 tsp raspberry jam

30 ml (1 fl. oz) lemon juice

60 ml (2 fl. oz) gin

1 tbsp simple syrup (see p. 20)

Ice cubes

1 Muddle together the raspberry jam and lemon juice until the jam starts to dissolve in the juice.

2 Stir in the gin and simple syrup.

3 Serve over ice.

Redcurrant jelly

I make jelly instead of jam with redcurrants and white currants because of their large, hard seeds. This very simple jelly is most often used to stick icing to cakes, or it can be tarted up with port to make Cumberland sauce. It goes excellently well with pâté, game and roast lamb. Don't bother to top and tail the berries as all the bits will be strained out. This recipe can be used for either redcurrants or white currants or for both together. Makes about 680 g (1½ lb).

900 g (2 lb) redcurrants

300 ml (½ pint) water

Sugar

1 Simmer the redcurrants over a low heat in the water until they are very soft.

2 Put in a clean, rinsed jelly bag and hang over a large bowl to drain. When all the juice has come out, measure the volume and put it in a preserving pan.

3 For every 600 ml (1 pint) of juice, add 450 g (1 lb) of sugar. Cook the mixture over a high heat until it reaches setting point (see p. 192). Watch out: it will boil up.

4 Pour into warm sterilised jars to within 6 mm (¼ inch) of the top, lid and seal.

Variation
Try adding a quarter to a half teaspoon of cinnamon and three cloves per 600 ml (1 pint) of juice when you add the sugar to add a spiced flavour.

Raspberry and blackcurrant jam

We sell a lot of this jam. The blackcurrants add a delicious sharpness to the raspberries for those who find raspberries a bit sweet. We cook the blackcurrants first as they are much tougher than the raspberries. Makes 3.4 kg (7½ lb).

1 kg (2¼ lb) blackcurrants

300 ml (½ pint) water

1 kg (2¼ lb) raspberries

2 kg (4½ lb) sugar

1 Put the blackcurrants and the water into a preserving pot. Cook over a low heat until the blackcurrants are soft and the skin smooshes to wee pieces between your fingers. This should take about 20 minutes.

2 Add the raspberries and cook until they start to lose their shape.

3 Add the sugar, stir well and then turn the heat up to full and cook the jam until it reaches setting point (see p. 195).

4 Pour into warm sterilised jars to within 6 mm (¼ inch) of the top, lid and seal.

Gooseberry and strawberry jam
I like gooseberry and strawberry jam. The gooseberries help the strawberries set quicker so it tastes fresher, and you don't need to add lemon. Use the recipe above, wtih half gooseberries and half strawberries, and cook the gooseberries first in the water.

TIP: To prepare raspberries (and related fruit), just pick over the fruit to remove any stems or hulls. Do not wash them unless they are really dirty, but if you do wash them, dry them off well and use them as soon as possible as they start growing mould very quickly. Try not to pick raspberries on a wet day, as by the time you get them home they may start to go mouldy; it's that fast. In fact, try not to pick any soft fruit in wet weather as the fruit can be watery, prone to mould and doesn't make the best jam.

Mixed summer berry jam

This is another of our award-winning jams: Silver at the 2014 Blas na hÉireann awards. It tastes summery and sharp and sweet, and, because the flavour is strong, it's a great jam for baking. It's also a good one to make at the end of the soft-fruit season when you only have a few handfuls of each type of berry. You need to watch the pot carefully because this combination can stick to the bottom and try to burn. Cook it on a much lower heat than usual and stir often. Makes about 3.4 kg (7½ lb).

---

500 g (18 oz) blackcurrants

500 g (18 oz) gooseberries

300 ml (½ pint) water

500 g (18 oz) strawberries (halved if large)

500 g (18 oz) raspberries

2 kg (4½ lb) sugar

1 Place the blackcurrants and gooseberries in a preserving pan with the water and cook over a low heat, stirring occasionally, until the berries soften and their skins smoosh to tiny pieces between your fingers.

2 Add the strawberries and raspberries and continue to cook over a low heat until they soften and begin to lose their shape. Stir a lot.

3 Add the sugar. Turn up the heat to medium high and cook the jam quickly, stirring often, until it reaches setting point (see p. 195).

4 Pour into warm sterilised jars to within 6 mm (¼ inch) of the top, lid and seal.

Variations
Substitute redcurrants or white currants for either the blackcurrants or gooseberries in the recipe.

Peach and raspberry summer smoothie

This tastes like a raspberry cake in drink form. The peaches add a silken sweetness. Serves 1.

2 ripe peaches (stoned and cut into chunks)

75 g (2½ oz) raspberries

200 ml (7 fl. oz) yogurt

¼ tsp vanilla extract

Honey

1 Blend peaches, raspberries, yogurt and vanilla extract together until smooth.

2 Taste and add honey if needed. (I find the peaches add enough sweetness for me.)

Nectarine jam

Imagine sitting in the warm morning sunshine eating nectarine jam on warm croissants. This is such a summery breakfast food. Use firm nectarines for this recipe. I don't remove the skins – I like the texture they give. Makes about 3.4 kg (7½ lb).

2 kg (4½ lb) stoned firm nectarines

150 ml (¼ pint) water

4 large lemons

2 kg (4½ lb) sugar

1 Cut the fruit into small, dice-sized pieces. Put in a preserving pan.

2 Add the water and the juice of the lemons to the pan and cook over a low heat, stirring occasionally, until the fruit softens (about 20 minutes).

3 Add the sugar, stir through and cook over a high heat, stirring occasionally, until the jam reaches setting point (see p. 195).

4 Pour into warm sterilised jars to within 6 mm (¼ inch) of the top, lid and seal.

Variations
You can use peaches or apricots instead of nectarines.

Prize-winning scones

These scones are the perfect partner to all your jams. When we moved to Ireland from America, Mom went to an ICA cookery demonstration and learned how to make scones and queen cakes, and then she taught us. We won lots of prizes in the local shows back when we were wee, and now my children make these scones and win prizes too. This recipe makes a light, soft, slightly crumbly scone. Eat them on the day they are made for the best taste and texture. I usually eat mine while they are still warm from the oven, with jam and cream. Makes 18 dainty scones.

2 eggs

300 ml (½ pint) milk

450 g (1 lb) plain flour

2 tsp baking powder

½ tsp salt

2 tbsp sugar

110 g (4 oz) butter

1 Preheat the oven to 200°C (400°F/Gas 6).

2 Beat the eggs in a measuring jug with enough milk to make 300 ml (½ pint) of liquid. You will have a little milk left over.

3 Put the dry ingredients in a bowl. Rub in the butter until the mixture resembles fine breadcrumbs. Add three-quarters of the liquid and mix well. If the mixture is too dry, add a bit more liquid or, if wet, add a bit more flour. You should have a soft dough that you can stick your finger through. (Don't over-handle the dough or the scones will be tough.)

4 Roll out the dough on a floured surface to 2.5 cm (1 inch) thick and cut into the desired shape. I use a 5-cm (2-inch) round cutter usually, but sometimes I cut the dough into squares or diamonds.

5 Place the scones on a lightly floured baking tray and then brush the top with the remaining egg and milk mixture. This gives them a nice shine and colour when they are cooked.

6 Bake for 10–15 minutes or until they are golden. Remove from the oven and leave to cool on a wire rack.

7 Spread with butter and jam and cream.

Variations
Add the zest of one lemon to the dry ingredients; or 2 tablespoons of raisins or sultanas; or ground cinnamon and the juice and zest of one orange. For savoury scones, leave out the sugar and add herbs or grated cheese.

Jam tarts

This is possibly the easiest pastry in the world and is often overlooked; however, a good jam tart filled with home-made jam is hard to beat. I use whatever jam, jelly or marmalade I have to hand, but be aware that if you use a runny jam the tart will be softer and will not keep as long. They last for about 4 days in an airtight container, but we like them best on the first day when the pastry is still crisp – either plain or served with a dollop of cream. Makes 12.

225 g (8 oz) plain flour

110 g (4 oz) butter (chopped)

Pinch of salt

6 tbsp cold water

225 g (8 oz) of jam

1 Put the flour in a bowl and rub in the butter until it resembles fine breadcrumbs. Add the salt and stir it through the mixture. Then add the water, a tablespoon at a time, until the dough sticks together. You may not need to use it all. Knead the dough a few times and then cover it and put it in the fridge to rest for at least 30 minutes.

2 Preheat the oven to 200°C (400°F/Gas 6) and get out a bun tin.

3 Roll the pastry out on a lightly floured surface to about 3 mm (⅛ inch) thick. Cut circles big enough to fill the holes in the bun tin. Place the circles in the tin, making sure there are no cracks in the pastry.

4 Put about 1 teaspoon of jam in each pastry case, filling them only half full. I know it looks very mingy and you might want to add more jam, but don't. The jam bubbles up as the tart cooks, and if you add any more it will bubble out of the pastry and all over the tin, making a burnt sticky mess.

5 Cook the tarts for 15–20 minutes until the pastry is golden. Remove from the oven and check that the tarts aren't stuck to the bun tin by moving them slightly. Let them finish cooling in the tin.

Batley cake

We made this teatime cake all the time when we were kids, and I still make it regularly. It's kind of like a soft vanilla shortbread with a layer of jam baked into it. You can use any jam you like, provided it's quite firm; otherwise it runs off the dough. This cake will freeze well and keeps for at least a week in an airtight container. Makes one 20-cm (8-inch) cake.

225 g (8 oz) plain flour

110 g (4 oz) butter

110 g (4 oz) sugar

1 tsp baking powder

1 egg

½ tsp vanilla essence

1 tbsp milk

3 tbsp firm jam (I like to use gooseberry)

1 tbsp icing sugar

1 Grease a 20-cm (8-inch) round cake tin and preheat the oven to 180°C (350°F/Gas 4).

2 Put the flour in a bowl and rub in the butter until the mixture resembles fine breadcrumbs. Stir in the sugar and baking powder.

3 Beat the egg, vanilla essence and milk together in a small bowl and then add to the dry ingredients. Blend together using a fork to form a soft dough.

4 Divide the dough into two and roll or pat out each piece into a 20-cm (8-inch) circle to fit the baking tin. Place one piece of the dough into the tin.

5 Using the back of a spoon, spread the jam over the dough in the tin to within a half inch of the edge. (If you spread it right up to the edge, the jam will escape out the sides, burn to the sides of the pan and make a mess.) Cover with the second round of dough.

6 Bake for around 50 minutes until well risen and golden brown. Leave to cool for about 10 minutes, then remove from the tin and leave to finish cooling on a wire rack.

7 Just before serving, sprinkle with icing sugar to make it pretty.

Cranachan

Who would have thought that just toasting oats would change them so much that they would go from a breakfast cereal to a star dessert? I make this for parties, and, since there is never any left, I guess my guests love it as much as I do. It's simple and quick, and you can pre-toast the oatmeal, then assemble the dessert in minutes. The oatmeal absorbs all the cream and raspberry juice, and it makes a lovely solid summer pudding. Some raspberries can be quite sour, so I always have extra honey for drizzling so everyone can sweeten their dessert to their own taste. Serves 2–3.

110 g (4 oz) porridge oats

450 g (1 lb) fresh raspberries

500 ml (17½ fl. oz) whipping cream

1 tbsp honey

1 tbsp whiskey

Garnish: more fresh raspberries and honey to serve

1 Toast the oats in a dry frying pan on a medium heat until they are light brown and start to smell nutty. Allow to cool.

2 While the oats are cooling, roughly crush the raspberries so the juice begins to run but there are still large pieces. (I use my mojito muddler for this.) Set aside.

3 Whip the cream until it is stiff and then fold the honey and whiskey through. Adjust to taste, making sure it is sweet enough and boozy enough.

4 Now fold the oats through the cream mixture.

5 In a glass dish, layer or swirl together the crushed raspberries and the cream mixture and leave this to set for a few minutes before serving. Garnish with fresh raspberries.

Variations
Try using Greek-style yogurt instead of cream for a more cheesecake-style dessert.

Sorbets and coulis 101

I make sorbets instead of ice creams – they are much simpler and healthier. For fruit you eat raw (strawberries, raspberries, peaches, apricots, nectarines, oranges and cherries), first purée the fresh fruit in a blender or food processor. You can strain the seeds and skin out, but I never bother because I like the texture. Taste it. Add enough sugar and lemon juice to make it delicious. (Start with half a lemon per 450 g/1 lb of fruit.) Make the purée sweeter than you would usually like as freezing can dull the sweetness. I add roughly 1 part sugar to 4 parts purée. Caster and icing sugar both dissolve easily. The sugar lowers the freezing point and allows little ice crystals to form. Without it, you would have a solid block of fruity ice. Pour the purée into a freezer-proof container and freeze for at least 4 hours. If your sorbet comes out of the freezer in a rock-hard lump – we all have bad recipe days – let it defrost on the counter and either eat it as it gets soft or add more sugar and refreeze it. If you want a sugar-free sorbet, freeze the prepared fruit on a baking tray and then pop the frozen pieces in a blender.

For fruit you eat cooked (blackcurrants, gooseberries, rhubarb, red and white currants, blueberries and blackberries), put the fruit in a medium-sized saucepan with a few tablespoons of water and cook over a low heat for a few minutes, until the fruit begins to soften and the juices begin to run. Remove from the heat, purée and leave to cool. Add enough sugar to sweeten to your taste. Pop it in a freezer-proof container and freeze for at least 4 hours.

Sorbets can be flavoured with herbs, spices, flowers and alcohol. Add a few sprigs of mint to blackcurrants while they are cooking, or three heads of elderflower to a batch of gooseberry purée for a wonderful earthy floral flavour. Stir a tablespoon or two of vodka into a blackcurrant sorbet before it goes into the freezer for a grown-up treat. Alcohol lowers the freezing point of the purée, so don't add too much or it will end up the consistency of a slushy. We eat our sorbets within a few days of making them for the freshest flavour.

A coulis is simply a sweetened smooth purée. Make a purée in the same way as for sorbet, then pass it through a strainer to remove any seeds. Sweeten to taste. Use less sugar than in a sorbet as it won't be frozen. A fruit coulis should keep for 3 days in the fridge.

Raspberry vinegar

Raspberry vinegar is the most popular of the fruit vinegars, but you can use this recipe for other soft fruits too. Use in vinaigrettes, in savoury sauces, on fruit salad and to tenderise meat. Add to mustard powder to make a fruity mustard. Add a splosh to iced water to make a refreshing summer drink. It should keep for at least a year in a cool dark cupboard. Makes about 900 ml (1½ pint).

---

450 g (1 lb) raspberries

600 ml (1 pint) distilled malt vinegar

Sugar

1 Place the berries in a glass or plastic container (not metal as the vinegar can cause metal to corrode) and mash lightly. Pour the vinegar over the berries.

2 Cover the container well (you don't want fruit flies getting into it) and leave it to sit for 2 weeks. Stir every day to make sure the vinegar pulls out as much flavour and colour as it can from the berries.

3 After 2 weeks, strain through a clean, rinsed jelly bag or a tightly woven cloth (don't squeeze it) until all the vinegar is out and the pulp left in the bag feels dry.

4 Measure the liquid and place in a preserving pan. For every 600 ml (1 pint) of liquid, add 225 g (8 oz) of sugar.

5 Bring the sweetened vinegar to the boil and cook over a medium heat for about 10 minutes.

6 Pour into warm sterilised bottles, lid and seal.

Variation
For a more delicate, perfumed flavour, use white wine vinegar instead of distilled malt vinegar.

Honeyed roast apricots

Fresh apricots remind me of the summer before college I spent at my grandma's in Utah. She had a tree in the backyard, laden with delicious, sun-ripened fruit. They can be grown here, in a very sunny sheltered area or in a polytunnel or greenhouse. Roasting apricots intensifies the flavour and colour, transforming slightly hard and bland apricots into a flavoursome joy. They can be eaten as a sweet or served with meats and go very well with pork and chicken. They can be kept for a few days in the fridge, if they last that long. Ours are usually devoured immediately.

Fresh apricots (3–4 per person)

Honey

Salt

1 Preheat the oven to 200°C (400°F/Gas 6).

2 Wash and dry the apricots and then split them lengthways and remove their pits.

3 Place the fruit, skin side down, in a shallow oven dish and fill the centres with honey (about half a teaspoon per apricot). Sprinkle a tiny pinch of salt on each apricot and bake for 10 minutes.

4 Take them out of the oven and leave to cool for a few minutes in the dish. Serve immediately, with cream or ice cream.

Variations
Roast apricots make a great breakfast food with yogurt and granola. Also, try them spread on toast and topped with chicken or cured ham, or have them with steak.

Growing apricots, nectarines and peaches

These all flower very early in the year so the blossoms are often destroyed by the frost. They need 5 months or so of frost-free growing for the fruit to ripen. Plant against a sunny south-facing wall or in the greenhouse or polytunnel. My nectarine tree grows happily in my polytunnel and produces a large crop of juicy delicious fruit every year. Keep well watered through the growing season.

Apricot cobbler

Cobbler originated in America as a replacement for the traditional English steamed suet pudding. I think it's a tasty improvement, and it's sure faster to make. It's one of my childhood favourites: crisp and sugary on top and velvety soft underneath. This recipe is specifically for firm sweet fruits you can eat raw: apricots, peaches, nectarines, plums, pears, eating apples or cherries. Don't use it for rhubarb or cooking apples. Makes one 23×8-cm (9×3inch) round dish (6 portions). Serve with cream or ice cream.

110 g (4 oz) butter

200 g (7 oz) sugar

110 g (4 oz) plain flour

1 tsp baking powder

250 ml (9 fl. oz) milk

450 g (1 lb) apricots (pitted and quartered)

1 Preheat oven to 180°C (350°F/Gas 4).

2 Melt the butter in the ovenproof dish you are going to cook the cobbler in.

3 Stir the sugar through the melted butter and then stir the flour and baking powder through this. It will resemble breadcrumbs.

4 Add the milk to the mixture and whisk until smooth.

5 Scatter the apricots across the top of the batter. It will look quite odd, but the batter will rise to cover the fruit.

6 Bake for 50–60 minutes until the top is golden brown and sugary crisp and it is cooked through. The bottom will be juicy and dense.

Variations
Add 60 g (2 oz) dark chocolate (yum!). Instead of chopping the fruit into bite-sized pieces, slice it thinly for a different texture. You could mix different fruit. Nectarines and apricots go very well together as do plums and blackberries. If you want to add berries, add only a few tablespoons as too much juice could cause the recipe to fail.

Coronation chicken

I first had this on a school field trip when we all traded lunches. I've loved this amazing curried chicken and peach salad ever since. I use a medium-hot curry as I want to taste the aromatic spices but don't want heat. I leave the skin on the peach, but you can peel it or just use a nectarine instead. It should hold for a few days in the fridge. Serves 2 as a salad or sandwich filling.

2 cooked chicken breasts (chopped into bite-size pieces)

1 large stalk of celery (finely chopped)

1 large ripe peach (chopped into dice-size pieces)

60 g (2 oz) flaked almonds

4 tbsp mayonnaise

1 tsp medium curry powder

Salt and pepper

1 Stir together the chicken, celery, peach (including any errant juice) and almonds.

2 Add the mayonnaise, stir again, then sprinkle the curry powder in and mix.

3 Taste the mixture, add salt and pepper and then taste again. Do you need a bit more curry powder? Is the mixture too dry? Do you need a bit more mayonnaise?

4 Leave it to sit in the fridge for at least an hour so the flavours blend together.

Moroccan date and nectarine chutney

I love when the nectarines are in season, mostly because I can make loads of this wonderful summer chutney, all spicy cinnamon and nectarine-sweet. It's my absolute favourite. I eat it with cheese, cold meats and chicken. You can substitute peaches for the nectarines as long as you peel them first. This is an adaptation of a recipe from *A Pickle and Chutney Cookbook*, by Digby Law, New Zealand's 'high priest of vegetables'. It keeps for at least 6 months. Makes 5.8 kg (13 lb).

3 kg (6½ lb) ripe nectarines (without their stones)

3 medium onions (finely chopped)

1 kg (2¼ lb) brown sugar

500 g (18 oz) dates (roughly chopped)

370 g (13 oz) raisins

10 cloves of garlic (peeled and sliced)

7.5 cm (3 inches) fresh ginger (grated)

1 tsp chilli flakes

1 tbsp cinnamon

1 tsp smoked paprika

2 tbsp salt

1.5 l (2½ pints) distilled malt vinegar

1 Chop the nectarines into dice-sized cubes. Put these and all the other ingredients into a preserving pot and bring to the boil over medium heat.

2 Reduce the heat and cook for about 1½–2 hours until it is thick and liquid begins to collect on the top.

3 Pour into warm sterilised jars or bottles to within 6 mm (¼ inch) of the top, lid and seal.

Nectarine parcels with brandy butter

This is one of my favourite summer recipes. You crack the top, scoop out the fruit pit and pop in a spoonful of brandy butter. As the butter melts, it mixes with the juices. Yum, yum, yum. The parcels can be left to cool, kept for a few days in the fridge and then reheated in the oven before serving. They can also be frozen. Serves 4.

PARCELS

225 g (8 oz) plain flour

110 g (4 oz) butter (chopped)

Pinch of salt

6 tbsp cold water

4 perfect nectarines or peaches (no blemishes)

3 tbsp milk (or egg and milk)

BRANDY BUTTER

90 g (3 oz) soft butter

1 tsp of vanilla extract

1 tbsp brandy

250 g (9 oz) icing sugar

Nutmeg or cinnamon

1 Put the flour in a bowl and rub in the butter until it resembles fine breadcrumbs. Add the salt and stir through. Then add the water, a tablespoon at a time, until the dough sticks together. You may not need to use it all. Knead it a few times, then cover and put in the fridge to rest for at least 30 minutes.

2 Preheat the oven to 200°C (400°F/Gas 6) and wash and dry the fruit.

3 Roll out the pastry on a lightly floured surface to 6 mm (¼ inch) thick and cut out circles double the circumference of the nectarines (use a saucer as a template).

4 Place a nectarine in the centre of a pastry circle, pull the pastry up around it and pinch it together at the top. The fruit should be completely sealed inside.

5 Put the nectarine parcels in a shallow baking dish. Brush with milk (or an egg and milk mixture) to give them a lovely golden sheen when baked. Bake for 40 minutes or until golden brown.

6 While the nectarines are cooking, make the brandy butter. Beat the butter, vanilla extract and brandy together.

7 Add enough icing sugar to make a thick sauce. A teaspoon should stand upright in the mixture. (You may not need all of the icing sugar.) I like mine so thick it's almost sliceable. Taste it and add more vanilla extract or brandy if needed.

8 Place the brandy butter in a serving bowl and then sprinkle nutmeg or cinnamon on top.

9 Remove the parcels from the oven, let them cool in their dish for a few minutes, and then serve with the brandy butter.

TIP: Always use perfect fruit. By doing this, you slow down the escape of the fruit juices, keeping more inside the pastry parcel.

Damn fine cherry pie

My homage to *Twin Peaks* is this 'damn fine pie'. The cherries are juicy and pop in your mouth, and the cherry almondy filling is thick and luscious. I have dreams about it. I tend to use a pastry lattice for my top crust so I can see all the gorgeous cherry filling – a feast for the eyes as well as the taste buds. Makes a 23-cm (9-inch) pie.

SHORTCRUST PASTRY

450 g (1 lb) plain flour

220 g (8 oz) butter (chopped)

Pinch of salt

12 tbsp cold water

PIE FILLING

625 g (22 oz) sweet cherries (pitted)

250 ml (9 fl. oz) water

3 tbsp cornflour

110 g (4 oz) sugar

1 tbsp lemon juice

Pinch of salt

¼ tsp almond essence

1 Put the flour in a bowl and rub in the butter until it resembles fine breadcrumbs. Add the salt and stir through, then add water, a tablespoon at a time, until the dough sticks together. You may not need to use it all. Knead it a few times and then cover and put in the fridge to rest for at least 30 minutes.

2 Put the cherries in a medium-sized saucepan with the water, cornflour, sugar, lemon juice and salt.

3 Stir well and cook over a medium heat for about 10 minutes, stirring occasionally to prevent sticking. The mixture should be thick enough to coat the back of a spoon. The juice should be pink and the cherries starting to soften slightly. Taste it and make sure it's sweet enough. Add more sugar if needed.

4 Remove from the heat and stir in the almond essence. Set aside to cool. If you don't leave the filling to cool before putting the top crust on, the pastry immediately starts to melt – and it's messy. (I speak from experience.)

5 Preheat the oven to 190°C (375°F/Gas 5).

6 Roll out half the pastry on a floured surface until it is about 3 mm (⅛ inch) thick and line a 20-mm (8-inch) pie dish with it. Fill with the cooled pie filling.

7 Roll out the rest of the pastry to 3 mm (⅛ inch) thickness and wide enough to cover the top of the pie. If you have a lattice cutter, cut slits in the pastry lid and then gently spread it across the top of the pie. Otherwise, cut a few slits to let the steam escape, along with those hot bubbly juices. Trim the excess pastry and crimp the pastry together.

8 Bake for 45 minutes until the filling starts to bubble up and the crust is golden brown. Leave to cool before serving. Serve with whipped cream or ice cream.

Chocolate cherry cake with cream-cheese frosting

Cherry-pie filling is not just for pies; we use it in this cake too. This is possibly the tastiest cake ever: almondy, chocolatey and full of cherry flavour. The cream-cheese icing is the perfect foil. Thanks are due to our pastry-chef friend, Corrin, for this recipe. It needs to be left to sit for a day before eating as it gets deliciously fudgy and dense. If you don't have the time, inclination or cherries to make the pie filling, just use a can. We make this cake in either a 23×33-cm (9×13 inch) cake pan or a 23×8-cm (9×3-inch) ring pan. Serves 12–16.

CAKE

110 g (4 oz) butter

310 g (11 oz) sugar

2 medium eggs

1 tsp almond essence

60 g (2 oz) cocoa powder

210 g (7½ oz) plain flour

1¼ tsp baking soda

1 tsp salt

595 g (21 oz) cherry-pie filling (see p. 92)

FROSTING

110 g (4 oz) full-fat cream cheese

110 g (4 oz) butter

1 tsp vanilla extract

400 g (14 oz) icing sugar

1 Preheat the oven to 180°C (350°F/Gas 4). Grease and flour the cake pan and set aside.

2 Cream together the butter and sugar until fluffy. Add the eggs and almond essence and mix again until well combined.

3 Add the cocoa powder, flour, baking soda and salt and beat until smooth. It will look very thick, but it'll be fine.

4 Carefully stir in the cherry-pie filling and then mix thoroughly.

5 Spread the batter evenly into the cake pan and bake for 45 minutes until just baked. Don't overcook as this will dry it out. Leave to cool for at least 3 hours before icing.

6 Cream together the cream cheese and butter, then add the vanilla extract. It might look a bit curdled at this stage, but the next step will fix that.

7 Add the icing sugar and mix again until smooth. It should be a good, spreadable consistency. If it's too thin, add a bit more sugar. If it's too thick, add a bit of milk – a half teaspoon at a time.

8 Cover the cake with the frosting and decorate with chocolate shavings and cherries.

TIP: Apply a very thin layer of icing to the outside of the cake and leave it to sit for a few hours. This is called the crumb layer, and it traps all the loose crumbs. Now put a second layer of icing over the outside of the cake and it should look pretty perfect.

Pod pasties

I grow a lot of mangetout and broad beans, and I'm always looking for ways to use them. You can use all mangetout, all broad beans, or add some regular peas. The oil-based pastry is very stretchy when raw and holds up well without crumbling when it's baked, ideal for pasties you want to eat from your hand – so great for packed lunches and picnics. These are crisp and delicious when straight out of the oven but are also great cold, from the fridge. Makes 32.

OIL PASTRY

225 ml (8 fl. oz) sunflower oil or mild olive oil

225 ml (8 fl. oz) water

1½ tsp salt

560 g (20 oz) plain flour

POD PESTO

250 g (9 oz) fresh, shelled broad beans

90 g (3 oz) fresh mangetout peas

60 g (2 oz) parmesan (roughly grated)

200 g (7 oz) ricotta (drained) or cottage cheese

½ lemon

¼ tsp ground black pepper

Salt

1 Combine the oil, water and salt in a bowl. Add two-thirds of the flour and mix well with a spoon. Gradually add in more of the flour until you get a soft dough that pulls away from the sides of the bowl and holds together in a ball.

2 Cover the bowl with cling film and leave to rest for half an hour at room temperature. Do not put in the fridge. If oil starts to come out of the dough, just knead it back in.

3 In a food processor, whizz up the beans and peas until they are roughly the size of cooked rice.

4 Add the parmesan and whizz to combine.

5 Add the ricotta, zest and juice of the half lemon and the pepper and whizz again. It should all start to stick together. Scrape down the sides of the bowl and whizz again.

6 Now taste it and add as much salt as you like. The parmesan can be very salty so you may not need to add any. The ricotta cheese can be quite sweet, so you may need to add another squeeze of lemon juice to balance the flavour.

7 Preheat oven to 190°C (375°F/Gas 5).

8 Make a ball of pastry about 2.5 cm (1 inch) across and roll it out flat to about 3 mm (⅛ inch) thick and about 10 cm (4 inches) across.

9 Put a teaspoon of the pod pesto in the middle of one half of the pastry circle and fold the other side of the pastry over it. Now pinch the pastry edges together. Carefully transfer to a baking tray. Repeat this process until all the pastry and filling are gone. You should have about 32 pasties. You can brush them with beaten egg or milk before baking to make them prettier.

10 Bake for 15 minutes until golden brown. Remove from the oven and leave to cool for a few minutes on the baking tray, then transfer to a wire rack to finish cooling.

Figs with cured ham

When I get the early season figs from the market, they don't even make it back home. I eat them straight out of their paper bag! We have some big old fig trees that can, on a good year, fruit very heavily, so I've added some fig recipes to my repertoire. These make an excellent light lunch dish or starter. The cured ham balances perfectly with the sweetness of the figs.

3 figs per serving (washed and dried)

2 slices air-dried ham (Parma, Serrano or Prosciutto) per fig

Balsamic vinegar

Olive oil

1 Slice the figs into quarters from the stem to about halfway down. Give a bit of a squeeze at the bottom to push the quarters apart slightly. You want the figs to sit upright. (You may have to take a little slice off the bottom.)

2 Wrap the base of the figs with the ham and place on the serving dish.

3 Drizzle with balsamic vinegar and olive oil.

Figs grilled with cheese

Goat's cheese and blue cheese both pair very well with figs, as they are usually salty and sour. For this recipe we grill the figs just enough to caramelise the skin and warm the cheese to release the flavours. Simple and delicious.

3 figs (washed and dried) per serving

1 tsp cheese (crumbly goat's cheese or blue cheese) per fig

Olive oil

Honey or balsamic vinegar

1 Slice the figs in quarters, from the stem to about halfway through.

2 Fill the middle with cheese, about a teaspoon depending on its size. (If the cheese is hard, slice it and slide the slices into the cuts in the fig.)

3 Place the figs in an ovenproof tray and brush them with a little olive oil.

4 Cook under a grill for a few minutes until the top of the fig is starting to brown and the cheese is softening.

5 Serve drizzled with honey or balsamic vinegar.

Fig tarts

These tarts are light and fresh and delicious. The slight sourness of the cream cheese sets off the sweetness of the figs, and the little sprinkle of dark chocolate brings all the flavours together. This is quite a sweet tart. If it's too sweet for your taste, reduce the amount of sugar or add a squeeze of lemon juice to the filling. Makes 6 small 10-cm (4-inch) tarts or one large 23-cm or 9-inch tart.

---

225 g (8 oz) plain flour

110 g (4 oz) butter (chopped)

½ tsp salt

6 tbsp cold water

250 ml (9 fl. oz) whipping cream

225 g (8 oz) cream cheese

200 g (7 oz) icing sugar

6 fresh figs (in 6-mm/¼-inch slices)

30 g (1 oz) dark chocolate shavings

1 Put the flour in a bowl and rub in the butter until it resembles fine breadcrumbs. Add the salt and stir through. Then add water, a tablespoon at a time, until the dough sticks together. You may not need to use it all. Knead a few times and then cover and put in the fridge to rest for at least 30 minutes.

2 Preheat the oven to 190°C (375°F/Gas 5).

3 Roll out the pastry on a floured surface until it is about 3 mm (⅛ inch) thick and line the tart cases with it. Prick the bottoms of the cases with a fork to stop the pastry from rising up.

4 Bake for 15–20 minutes until golden brown. Remove from the oven and leave to cool.

5 Whip the cream until it forms stiff peaks. Beat the cream cheese and icing sugar together until smooth as silk, then fold in the whipped cream.

6 Now fill the cold pastry cases with the cream-cheese mixture.

7 Cover with the sliced figs, sprinkle with the chocolate shavings and serve immediately.

Variation
You can replace the figs with any fresh sliced fruit.

Growing figs

Fig trees grow very well here, but in order to get them to fruit well you need to keep their roots restricted (to stop lots of leafy growth) and plant them in a sunny and sheltered place such as a greenhouse, polytunnel or against a south-facing wall.

Lamb and fig tagine

This is my absolute favourite meal, and I've been having it for my birthday dinner for more years than I can count. I love the lightly spiced lamb, the sweetness of the figs and the crunch of the almonds. I cut the figs into halves rather than quarters as they hold together during the cooking and look better when served. It also works well with apricots, peaches or nectarines instead of the figs. Serve with bulgar or couscous. Makes enough for 3–4.

2 tbsp olive oil

500 g (18 oz) lamb (cubed)

2 medium onions (finely sliced)

2 cloves of garlic (finely chopped)

1 cm (½ inch) fresh ginger (grated)

½ tsp ground cinnamon

½ tsp cumin seeds

½ tsp turmeric powder

1 tsp ground paprika

½ tsp whole black peppercorns

½ tsp coriander seed

Pinch of freshly grated nutmeg

500 ml (17½ fl. oz) water

½ tsp salt

1 tbsp tomato purée

110 g (4 oz) whole blanched almonds

1 tsp honey or more to taste

4 fresh figs (cut in half)

Optional: juice of ½ lemon, natural yogurt, fresh chopped mint and fresh chopped coriander

1 Heat the olive oil in a heavy saucepan, then fry the lamb and onions over a medium heat for a few minutes until they are brown and the onions are starting to stick to the bottom of the pot.

2 Add the garlic and spices to the pot and stir them through. Fry this for only a minute – just to warm the spices. (It's going to try and stick, so stir well.)

3 Then add the water and quickly stir it through.

4 Add in the salt, tomato purée and almonds and leave to cook, covered, over a low heat for an hour.

5 Add the honey and figs and cook for another 25 minutes or until the lamb is tender and the stew has thickened.

6 Taste and add a squeeze of lemon juice if it's sweeter than you like or a bit more honey if you'd like it sweeter. Remove from the heat and garnish with yogurt, mint and coriander.

Cucumber stew

We all have those days in summer when you can't face another salad. Maybe it's rainy or overcast or you just need something good and hearty. I got this recipe from my friend Cathy back when my kids were little. We had a gazillion cucumbers taking over my polytunnel, and the kids simply couldn't eat another slice of fresh cucumber. I don't know why I had never thought of cooking them, because I cook courgettes and they are similar. Cathy assured me it was delicious, so we gave it a try – and she was so right. It's fresh-tasting but also very filling. Makes 3–4 servings.

1 tbsp olive oil

1 medium onion (finely chopped)

1 large potato (peeled and cut into 1-inch cubes)

2 large cucumbers (peeled, deseeded and cut into 1-inch cubes)

900 ml (1½ pints) vegetable stock

1 tbsp plain flour

1 tbsp soft butter

Salt and pepper

Garnish: chopped fresh mint or other summer herbs and either fresh cream, yogurt or sour cream

1 In a large saucepan, heat the olive oil over a medium heat and add the onion. Cook for a few minutes until translucent, stirring occasionally.

2 Add the potato and cucumber. Cook until they are just starting to turn golden brown along the edges.

3 Add the stock and cook over a medium heat for about 20 minutes, stirring occasionally, until the cucumber and potatoes are tender. Remove from the heat.

4 Mash the flour and butter together in a bowl, then whisk this into the stew to thicken it.

5 Put the stew back on the heat and bring it to the boil for a minute to cook up the flour.

6 Remove from the heat, taste and season with salt and pepper. Garnish with some fresh mint or other summer herbs. Add either a drizzle of fresh cream, a dollop of yogurt or a spoon of sour cream. Serve with hot crusty bread. Yum.

Variations
To make a chicken version, replace the vegetable stock with chicken stock and add two chopped cooked chicken breasts to the finished stew. If you would like a gluten-free stew, use either cornflour, a carton of crème fraiche or yogurt to thicken the stew instead of flour.

Cucumber pickle

This fridge pickle won't keep for more than a week but is a delicious way of using cucumbers. Even my cucumber-hating husband loves it! We use it as a side salad and also on sandwiches. Use a mandolin slicer if you have one to get very thin slices. I sometimes jazz it up by adding thinly sliced fresh beetroot (which gives it a bright pink colour) or a tablespoon of fresh dill or fennel. Makes 4 salad servings.

1 large cucumber (thinly sliced)

1 medium onion or large shallot (thinly sliced)

6 tbsp sugar

4 tbsp white vinegar

1 tsp salt

½ tsp cracked black peppercorns

1 Put the cucumber and onion in a bowl and stir together.

2 Mix the sugar, vinegar, salt and pepper together to make a paste. Pour this over the cucumber mixture and stir well.

3 Cover and pop it in the fridge. It will look like you've just covered the cucumber in sugar, but leave it for a few hours and the sugar and salt will have pulled water out of the cucumber to make a pickling juice and it will be ready to eat.

Cordials and syrups 101

I like to make my own cordials and syrups as I can be sure what ingredients there are in them and can control the sugar content. It's also much cheaper. Cordials and syrups are both sweetened syrups, but while cordials are diluted with water, syrups are used undiluted. A syrup needs to be quite sweet, but a cordial can be less so. I find it's the colour and berry flavour my kids love more than the sweetness.

Making cordials and syrups is very straightforward. Simply cook the fruit in enough water to cover, strain and sweeten to taste. We use regular white granulated sugar, but you can use cane sugar, brown sugar, honey or even stevia although they will all affect the flavour. If you use honey, heat it only enough to let the honey dissolve (to preserve its health-giving properties). I sometimes add lemon juice to cordials along with the sugar just to sharpen the fruit flavour.

Dilute the cordials in water (sparkling or still) for a refreshing drink. Add to white wine or champagne or use in cocktails. We use ours as syrups on waffles, pancakes and ice cream and add them to milk for simple milkshakes. You can also use them to moisten cakes when making desserts like shortcake or trifle. Freeze diluted cordial to make ice lollies.

You don't want a bland cordial or syrup, so use good strong flavours. Combinations like raspberry and blackcurrant or strawberry, raspberry, blackcurrant and gooseberry all work well. Gooseberry and elderflower is another great combination. You may have to freeze the elderflowers as they are ready about a month before the gooseberries. I use about two heads of elderflowers per 450 g (1 lb) of gooseberries.

Try a rhubarb cordial, plain or with ginger or coriander. Add an inch of fresh ginger or a teaspoon of cracked coriander seeds to each 450g (1 lb) of rhubarb. For apple and cinnamon cordial, use about 1 teaspoon of cinnamon powder per 1.8 l (3 pints) of apple juice – add it with the sugar. Elderberry syrup is not only delicious but it is reputed to be antiviral. I feed it to the family when they have a flu coming on. It's also our favourite pancake syrup.

Blackcurrant cordial

I make loads of this during the summer when the blackcurrants are in season. My kids' tongues seem permanently stained purple. Sugar is used here as a flavouring rather than as a preservative – it will only last about a week in the fridge and may start to ferment if you keep it longer. You can freeze it in plastic containers (washed milk and cream bottles are perfect). Remember to leave a bit of room for expansion. From 600 ml (1 pint) of juice and 225 g (8 oz) sugar, you will get about 650 ml (23 fl. oz) of cordial.

1 kg (2¼ lb) blackcurrants

Water

Sugar

1 Don't bother to top and tail the blackcurrants. Place them in a preserving pan and add enough water to just cover the fruit. (I find I usually use about 1.2 l (2 pints).

2 Cook over a low heat until the fruit breaks down and smooshes between your fingers. You cook it this long to extract as much colour and flavour as you can. This can take up to an hour.

3 Place the cooked blackcurrants in a rinsed jelly bag and let drain into a large bowl or pot until the pulp is dry and no more juice drips out of the bag. Overnight should be long enough. If you can't wait that long, squeeze the jelly bag to get as much juice out as possible. Prepare to have purple-stained hands for a day though.

4 Measure the juice, put it into a large pot and start to warm on a low heat. Taste it and add about half the amount of sugar that you think you'll need. I use 225 g (8 oz) of white granulated sugar per 600 ml (1 pint) of juice as that's what suits our palates.

5 Cook over a low heat, stirring occasionally, until the sugar is dissolved. Taste it and add more sugar, a tablespoonful at a time, until it's as sweet as you want. You don't want to over-sweeten it. Continue to cook over that low heat until all the sugar is dissolved. (Keep stirring it once in a while.) This doesn't take very long, about 5–10 minutes. Remove the pot from the heat and let it cool.

6 Pour the cordial into storage containers, seal and pop in the fridge.

Variation
For a slightly more adult cordial, add a few sprigs of fresh mint to the pot with the sugar and let the fresh mint flavour infuse through. Take the mint out when the cordial is cool.

Mellow Fruitfulness

Blueberry muffins

There's no better breakfast than hot muffins straight from the oven. These are American-style breakfast muffins, best eaten within a few hours of baking, slathered in butter. This recipe is an adaptation of one from my much loved and falling apart copy of *The Better Homes and Gardens Cookbook*. I also make them with blackberries or raspberries. Makes 12.

200 g (7 oz) plain flour

75 g (2½ oz) sugar

2 tsp baking powder

¼ tsp cinnamon

Large pinch of salt

110 g (4 oz) blueberries

1 egg

170 ml (6 fl. oz) milk

60 ml (2 fl. oz) sunflower oil

¼ tsp vanilla essence

½ lemon

6 tsp coarse brown sugar (for sprinkling)

1 Preheat oven to 200°C (400°F/Gas 6). Line a 12-muffin pan with paper baking cases.

2 Collect three bowls. In one bowl put the flour, sugar, baking powder, cinnamon and salt. Stir together.

3 Put the blueberries in the second bowl. Take 2 tablespoons of the flour mixture from the first bowl and mix it through the berries. This prevents them sinking to the bottom of the muffins by soaking up some of the berry juice as they cook.

4 In the third bowl, beat the egg, milk, sunflower oil, vanilla essence and coarsely grated zest and juice of the half lemon. Add this to the first bowl with the dry ingredients.

5 Stir until everything is just barely mixed together – enough so you can't see any dry ingredients. The batter should still be lumpy. Over-mixing makes muffins tough. Now, carefully fold in the blueberries.

6 Divide the batter evenly between the cases and sprinkle a thin layer of sparkly sugar (about half a teaspoon) on each.

7 Bake for about 15–20 minutes until well risen and golden brown.

Growing blueberries

Blueberries need an acid soil, so if you don't have this you need to grow them in large containers or in a raised bed filled with a peat-moss-based ericaceous soil. Blueberries crop very well, and the berries don't all ripen at once so you can pick for a few weeks. For blueberry jam, use the recipe for raspberry jam on p. 66.

Mustikkapiirakka (Finnish blueberry pie)

This is actually a sweet yeast cake bread, not a pie. Have it for tea! This recipe is from my friend Katrina, whose mom is Finnish. It takes a bit of time to make, but it's so worth it. Hot, bubbly blueberries on a soft cardamom-flecked bread are wonderful. Make it with fraughans (wild blueberries) if you can find them. They are very fiddly to pick but are well worth the effort. Makes a 25-cm (10-inch) cake and 6–8 servings.

60 g (2 oz) sugar

60 g (2 oz) soft butter

¼ tsp ground cardamom seeds

1 tsp salt

125 ml (4½ fl. oz) warm milk

125 ml (4½ fl. oz) hand-hot water

1 tbsp active dried yeast

1 egg (beaten)

480 g (1 lb 1 oz) plain flour

450 g (1 lb) blueberries

2 tbsp sugar

2 tbsp cornflour

Zest of 1 lemon (if you are using cultivated blueberries)

1 Put the sugar, butter, cardamom and salt into a large bowl. Add the milk and stir with a whisk until well blended.

2 Mix the hand-hot water and yeast together and slowly add to the milk mixture, stirring all the time. Add the egg.

3 Put half the flour into the bowl of liquids and blend it in. Then add the rest in four stages, until the dough holds together but is still soft.

4 Take the dough out of the bowl and knead it for at least 5 minutes until it is smooth and the surface springs back when poked with your finger. Grease a large bowl and place the dough in it. Cover with cling film or a tea towel and let rise for about an hour in a warm place until it doubles in size. Punch this down to let the air out and let it rest for another 15 minutes. Now it's ready to use.

5 Preheat the oven to 190°C (375°F/Gas 5) and grease a 25-cm (10-inch) pie dish or cake pan.

6 Fill the pan with the dough as if you were making a pizza. Push the dough up the sides of the dish to create a space in the centre for the filling.

7 Mix the blueberries, sugar, cornflour and lemon zest (if using) in a bowl, then pour into the centre of the dough.

8 Bake for about 45 minutes or until the filling is bubbling and the pastry is risen and golden brown. Leave to cool for at least 10 minutes before serving as the molten blueberries can give a nasty mouth burn. (I know: I was too greedy to wait.)

Silver-dollar blackberry pancakes

Early in August, just as the first few blackberries ripen, I can be seen down my boreen in my PJs, picking berries for breakfast pancakes. To me, they're the taste of August and the start of the harvest. These are American-style pancakes and are called 'silver dollar' because they are about the size of an old silver dollar, about 6 cm (2½ inches) across. Serve with butter, maple syrup, jam, jelly, cream – whatever takes your fancy. It's my son Alex's recipe. Makes 16–18.

250 ml (9 fl. oz) milk

½ lemon (1 tbsp juice and, separately, the finely grated zest)

1 egg

140 g (5 oz) plain flour

1 tbsp sugar

¼ tsp salt

1 tsp baking powder

¼ tsp baking soda

1 tsp vanilla essence

2 tbsp melted butter (slightly cooled)

170 g (6 oz) blackberries

1 Mix the milk and lemon juice together and let this sit for 5 minutes. (This sours the milk.)

2 Separate the egg and beat the white until it forms soft peaks.

3 In a mixing bowl, stir together the flour, sugar, salt, baking powder, baking soda and lemon zest.

4 Add the soured milk next, then the vanilla essence and the egg yolk. Stir this all together until just combined – it should still be a bit lumpy. Now stir in the melted butter.

5 Fold in the egg whites carefully and mix again until just combined. Finally, fold in the blackberries. Now it's ready to cook.

6 Place a heaped tablespoon of batter onto a heated and greased frying pan and cook over a medium to low heat until the bubbles that appear on the top of the pancake all burst (about 1–2 minutes). Now flip the pancake over and cook the other side until it is golden. Done.

Blackberry lore

Blackberries have been eaten since the earliest times and were listed as one of the 'bushes of the wood' in the Brehon laws. If you cleared a field of brambles you were fined the price of a one-year-old heifer – they were that valuable. They were often used to make wreaths for cow byres to protect the cows from the evil eye and witchcraft.

Tomato and goat's cheese tarts

We have these tarts quite often in the summer when I'm harvesting gazillions of deliciously sweet cherry tomatoes from the greenhouse. I usually buy puff pastry as it's almost as good as home-made and because I seldom have the time or inclination to make it from scratch. (Bought puff pastry comes in lots of different sizes so adjust the recipe to suit.) I use a green basil pesto, but you can try it with smoked sundried tomato pesto or any kind of pesto you have. If I have pine nuts in the house, they finish the dish perfectly. Makes 9 tarts.

500 g (18 oz) package of puff pastry

2–3 tbsp (heaped) pesto

200 g (7 oz) cherry tomatoes (halved or quartered)

200 g (7 oz) log of soft goat's cheese (sliced into 6-mm/¼-inch rounds)

1 tbsp pine nuts (optional)

1 Preheat the oven to 200°C (400°F/Gas 6).

2 Roll out the puff pastry until it is about 3 mm (⅛ inch) thick. Cut into 9 equal pieces (as square as possible) and then score a square with a knife 2.5 cm (1 inch) inside the edge of each piece, cutting halfway through the dough.

3 Inside this scored square, spread about half a teaspoon of pesto.

4 Divide the tomatoes and cheese between the tarts. Sprinkle a few pine nuts on each, if you are using them.

5 Place the tarts onto a baking sheet and bake for 20 minutes, until the cheese is melted and the pastry is risen and golden brown.

6 Take the tarts out of the oven and let cool for at least 5 minutes before serving.

Variations

If you don't like goat's cheese, you can substitute mozzarella or even cheddar.

Tomato salsa

Is salsa a salad, a sauce or a dip? I use it as all of these things. I make it chunky when using it as a salad and a bit smoother when it's needed for a thick sauce or dip. I add it to breakfast eggs, pile it on burgers, use it for nachos, slather it on falafels and tacos, and I always have it on the side at barbeques. It's fast to make and adds a blast of fresh flavour to your meal. I usually make this in a food processor, but it's fine to chop everything by hand – just make sure the pieces of onion are smaller than everything else. No one wants a mouthful of onion! Serves 8.

1 medium onion

450 g (1 lb) fresh tomatoes (quartered if large)

1 sweet yellow, green or red pepper (deseeded and quartered)

¼ tsp dried chilli flakes or ½ tsp chopped fresh chilli

1 good handful of fresh coriander (roughly chopped)

Juice of 1 lemon

3 medium cloves of garlic (finely chopped)

Salt and pepper

1 Place the onion in the food processor and pulse a few times until it is in pea-sized pieces.

2 Add the rest of the ingredients and pulse a few times until the mixture is the consistency you want. I like the pieces to be around the size of kidney beans for salad, but smaller for a dip.

Variations

Substitute lime juice for the lemon and add half a teaspoon of cumin. If you don't have fresh coriander, use parsley or just leave it out. It will still be good. Substitute a can of tomatoes for fresh tomatoes if it's more convenient. (The salsa will be more runny.)

Tomato tapenade

I love this tomato tapenade for its intense flavour. We use it hot on fresh pasta or cold on small toasts or rustic bread. We also use it as a fancy pizza sauce. It keeps in the fridge for at least 3 days. If you don't have fresh tomatoes, a can of good plum tomatoes will do. Makes about 350 ml (12 fl. oz).

3 tbsp olive oil

6 cloves garlic (chopped)

1 small onion (finely chopped)

1 tbsp dried oregano

1 tsp dried basil

¼ tsp chilli flakes

400 g (14 oz) fresh tomatoes (roughly chopped)

Salt and pepper

1 Heat the oil in a frying pan. Add the garlic and onion and cook over a medium heat for about 3 minutes, until the onion is slightly soft.

2 Add the oregano, basil and chilli and mix through.

3 Add the tomatoes and stir well.

4 Lower the heat and simmer until the tomatoes start to soften and their pulp and juices combine with the oil to give a gorgeous sauce. This can take anything from 20 to 40 minutes.

5 Taste and add as much salt and pepper as you feel it needs.

Variations
Add a splosh of red wine or vinegar just before the end of cooking to give an extra-sharp flavour. Try adding some black olives or red peppers to the mix for a bit more variety.

Zucchini bread (courgette cake)

This is an excellent sweet cake bread, similar to carrot cake, and very quick and easy to make. Even vegetable-hating kids love it! When we were little, it was one of Mom's most requested market cakes. I always make it in buns for our summer parties as they are so handy, and they are tasty too. I serve the larger loaf size sliced and buttered. It freezes well. The recipe makes one large loaf pan (23×13×8 cm/9×5×3 inch) or 14–16 muffin-size buns.

---

2 eggs

170 ml (6 fl. oz) vegetable oil

250 g (9 oz) sugar

1¼ tsp vanilla essence

200 g (7 oz) courgette (grated, but leave the skin on)

250 g (9 oz) plain flour

1 tsp bread soda

½ tsp salt

½ tsp baking powder

1 tsp cinnamon

½ tsp nutmeg

90 g (3 oz) raisins

60 g (2 oz) chopped nuts

1 Preheat the oven to 160°C (325°F/Gas 3).

2 Beat together eggs, oil, sugar and vanilla essence until well mixed and thick.

3 Stir in the grated courgette.

4 Add the remaining ingredients and mix until well combined. The batter will look sloppy, but that's the way it should be.

5 Put into the baking pan or pans and bake for approximately 25–30 minutes (for buns) and about 1 hour (for larger breads), until a skewer inserted into the cake comes out clean.

Variations
You can substitute grated apple for the courgette to make apple bread. I also saw a recipe that added 6 g (2 oz) of chocolate chips to the mix. Yum!

Courgette and ginger jam

If you've grown courgettes, you'll know that towards the end of the summer you have more than you know what to do with. You've added them to every meal and have foisted them off on your friends (who now hide when they see you coming). So now it's time to make jam. This jam is a bright sunshine yellow with green flecks and tastes like summer. I eat it for breakfast on toast or scones and also use it in curries or on poppadoms. You can use either tiny courgettes or the monster you found lurking behind the leaves. Makes 4.5 kg (10 lb).

2.7 kg (6 lb) prepared courgette

10 cm (4 inches) fresh ginger (peeled and roughly chopped)

4 lemons

1.8 l (3 pints) water

2.7 kg (6 lb) sugar

1 Scratch the skin off the courgette with your thumbnail. If it comes away easily, it doesn't need peeling. Otherwise, remove the skin. Remove any large, hard seeds and roughly chop the flesh.

2 Whizz the courgette and ginger in a food processor until they are in rice-sized pieces and then place in a large preserving pan.

3 Wash and quarter the lemons and then whizz them in the food processor until they are puréed. Add to the pan and then add the water.

4 Cook over a medium heat, stirring occasionally, until the courgette is translucent (about 40 minutes).

5 Add the sugar to the pan and mix thoroughly. Continue cooking on a medium heat, stirring constantly, until the sugar dissolves. Then turn the heat up to high and cook, stirring only occasionally, until the jam reaches setting point.

6 Pour into warm sterilised jars to within 6 mm (¼ inch) of the top, lid and seal.

Roast pepper butter

For years I'd heard about roast peppers and had thought, *Roast peppers? How good can they possibly be?* Fantastic is how good. Roast pepper butter captures that flavour and makes a versatile spread, condiment or sauce. I only use red peppers for this recipe as green ones can be a wee bit bitter and not the flavour I want and because yellow peppers give the flavour but not the colour (which is part of the joy of this butter). I use this as a spread on bread, to season vegetables and baked potatoes and on fish and meat (especially barbecued meat). Makes approximately 340 g (12 oz).

1 medium red bell pepper or any sweet pepper

225 g (8 oz) softened butter

Flaked sea salt and pepper

1 Preheat oven to 200°C (400°F/Gas 6).

2 Wash the pepper well and put it (stem, seeds and all) in an oven dish. Roast uncovered for at least 20 minutes – until the skin starts to blacken. Take out of the oven and leave to cool.

3 Then peel off the skin and remove the stem and seeds. Keep all the juice – you want that flavour.

4 Put the pepper and its juices in a food processor and whizz until it's a smooth purée.

5 Add the butter and whizz until it's smooth.

6 Taste it and season with salt and pepper. I like the crunch of flaked sea salt in this recipe.

7 Pop it into a bowl and put in the fridge to harden back up.

TIP: Roll the butter into a sausage about 5 cm (2 inches) in diameter and wrap it in cling film. Leave it to harden back up and then slice rounds for serving. You can also freeze it (for about 3 months).

Apple jelly

I start making apple jelly as soon as the first unripe apples fall from the trees in August. The eating varieties are still green and sour and have plenty of acid and pectin. As the season progresses, the eating apples ripen and get sweeter, so I mix them with cooking varieties, which are still sour. You cannot make a good apple jelly from sweet eating apples only; the jelly won't set properly. Always add sour apples to the pot – a maximum of 1 part eating to 3 part cookers. At the end of the season, the cooking apples start to mature and soften and sweeten slightly so I don't add any eaters at all. I also make a lot of crab-apple jelly from both wild and cultivated crabs. When making crab-apple jelly, I mix cooking apples with the crab apples 50/50 as I find pure crab-apple jelly too tongue-furringly sour for my taste. Makes 4.5 kg (10 lb).

3.5–4.5 kg (8–10 lb) washed apples (whatever fits in your pot)

Water

Sugar

1 Roughly chop the unpeeled and uncored apples and place them in a large preserving pan. Add enough cold water to just cover them. (Push the apples down with your hand to judge how much is needed.)

2 Cook on a medium to high heat for about 45 minutes until the flesh has gone to pulp and the skin has started to disintegrate. The apples will start to swell up as they cook and will try to escape the pot so watch them and keep pushing them back down.

3 Put the apple pulp in a clean rinsed jelly bag and leave to drain above a large bowl for at least an hour if not overnight. The longer you drain, the more juice you get, but I find that most of it is out within an hour.

4 Measure the juice. This amount of apples usually produces around 3.4 l (6 pints). Pour into a clean preserving pan with 450 g (1 lb) of sugar for every 600 ml (1 pint) of juice. The juice will be cloudy, but adding the sugar and heating will clear it.

5 Cook up the jelly on a high heat. It may take anything from 20–40 minutes until it reaches setting point (see p. 192).

6 Pour into warm sterilised jars to within 6 mm (¼ inch) of the top, lid and seal.

Variations
Make a few different flavours from a single batch. Add five cloves, a large pinch of cinnamon or a quarter teaspoon of dry rosemary, mint or chilli to each 225 g or 8-ounce jar.

Lamb chops with apple jelly

One of my favourite and simplest recipes is to spread lamb chops with a spoonful of apple jelly before grilling or pan-frying. The jelly caramelises and adds a wonderful sweet fruitiness to the meat. I finish by garnishing the cooked chop with another spoonful of jelly. Try it with pork chops too.

Quince jelly

Quinces are hard and yellow, the wonderfully perfumed relation of apples and pears. They taste completely unlike any other fruit: delicate and perfumed. True quinces (*Cydonia*) grow on a tree similar to apple, take years to fruit and are not very widely planted, but there is a fairly common ornamental bush called *Japonica quince* (*Chaenomeles*) which produces a similar fruit that can also be used in jelly. If you are lucky enough to grow or find some, make apple and quince jelly – it's a delight. It pairs very well with cheese and pâté but really comes into its own with goose, pork or duck. Use the apple jelly recipe, but replace half the apples with quince. Cut the pieces of quince half the size of the pieces of apple as the quince is a very hard fruit and you want both to cook at roughly the same rate.

Apple jelly cocktail

60 ml (2 fl. oz) whiskey

1 tsp apple jelly

¼ tsp grated fresh ginger

¼ tsp ground ginger

Pinch of grated nutmeg

90 ml (3 fl. oz) cider

Ice cubes

1 Mix together the whiskey, jelly and spices.

2 Leave to sit for 10 minutes until the jelly starts to dissolve.

3 Add the cider and serve over ice.

Apple-pie filling

This filling isn't just for apple pies. You can use it for strudel, crumbles, turnovers or even sandwich-toaster sandwiches. It is also great on porridge or overnight oats. I would advise making a double batch as it's so tasty you'll want a second pie straight after you've finished the first. This makes enough filling for a 23-cm (9-inch) apple pie. It will keep for a few days in the fridge and in the freezer for at least a month.

90 g (3 oz) brown sugar

110 g (4 oz) white sugar

Juice of 1 lemon

1¼ tsp cinnamon

¼ tsp nutmeg

¼ tsp ground cloves (optional)

½ tsp vanilla essence (optional)

Pinch of salt

4 tbsp cornflour

500 ml (17½ fl. oz) water

1 kg (2¼ lb) peeled and cored sour eating apples (chopped into 2.5-cm/1-inch cubes)

1 Put the sugars, lemon juice, spices, vanilla essence (if using), salt and cornflour in a large, heavy-bottomed saucepan.

2 Cook on a medium heat, uncovered, for a few minutes until the ingredients turn into a thick syrup and start to bubble.

3 Stir the water into the syrup mixture and cook for 2 minutes, stirring constantly, until it starts to thicken.

4 Add the chopped apple and stir it through.

5 Reduce the temperature to low and cook for about 10 minutes, stirring to prevent it sticking, until the apples just begin to soften. You don't want them to disintegrate. Remove from the heat and leave to cool.

Variations
This tastes like classic American pie filling, but if you'd like to play with the flavours, try adding ground coriander, ginger, allspice or cardamom.

Serving suggestions
For an apple pie, put the filling in an unbaked pie crust, cover with streusel topping (see p. 41) and bake at 200°C (400°F/Gas 6) for 30–40 minutes until golden and bubbly. For crumble, put the filling in a casserole dish and top with streusel, adding 60 g (2 oz) porridge oats for a crunchier crumble topping. Bake for 30 minutes at 180°C (350°F/Gas 4) until it is golden and bubbly.

Apple chutney

This is the first chutney I learned to make. It's simple, and it goes with everything. We use it with cheese, burgers, pies and sausages, in cream cheese for dips and on the side with our curries. Use the biggest cooking apples you can find as it's a nuisance to peel smaller ones. Keeps for at least 6 months unopened in its jar. Makes about 6.8 kg (15 lb).

3.6 kg (8 lb) peeled, cored and diced cooking apples

900 g (2 lb) onions

1.2 l (2 pints) distilled malt vinegar

900 g (2 lb) brown sugar

450 g (1 lb) sultanas or raisins

2 tsp ground ginger

2 tbsp salt

2 tbsp whole yellow mustard seed

½ tsp cayenne pepper or chilli powder

1   Put the apples in a preserving pan. Peel and finely chop the onions and add to the pan. Add the rest of the ingredients and mix well.

2   Bring the mixture to boil over a medium heat, stirring occasionally, and when it starts to bubble turn the heat down to low and leave it to simmer, stirring occasionally, for about 1½–2 hours.

3   The chutney is ready when it has thickened and has darkened in colour, the apple has all disintegrated, and liquid begins to float on top. It should also have reduced by about a third.

4   Remove from the heat and pour into warm sterilised jars to within 6 mm (¼ inch) of the top, lid and seal.

Curried date and apple chutney
Substitute 1 tablespoon of medium-hot curry powder for the spices, replace the raisins with 500 g (18 oz) dates and add 8 chopped cloves of garlic and 1 tablespoon of treacle. I have my friend Katrina to thank for this spicy and rich version.

Apple-pie cake

This is another of Mom's market cake recipes and the one she insisted go in this book as it's so good. It's so cinnamony, appley and yummy and is good either warm or cold. We eat it with ice cream or whipped cream as a dessert or with big chunks of cheddar cheese as an anytime snack. Sometimes we have it for breakfast. (Don't judge me!) Makes one 23-cm (9-inch) pie cake and serves 4–6.

60 g (2 oz) butter

140 g (5 oz) sugar

1 egg (slightly beaten)

110 g (4 oz) plain flour

1 tsp baking soda

1 tsp ground cinnamon

½ tsp salt

½ tsp ground nutmeg

⅛ tsp ground cloves

1 tsp vanilla essence

60 g (2 oz) chopped pecans or walnuts (optional)

2 medium eating apples (cored and diced) – about 2 cups

1 Preheat the oven to 180°C (350°F/Gas 4) and grease a 23-cm (9-inch) pie dish.

2 Melt the butter and pour into a large mixing bowl. Add the sugar and egg and mix with a spoon until well combined.

3 Mix in the rest of the ingredients. (It will look like there is way too much apple, but that's fine.)

4 Spoon the batter into the pie dish and carefully flatten it out – it's very lumpy and sticky.

5 Bake for 40–5 minutes. Remove from the oven, cool and serve straight from the pie dish.

Growing apples

Research what varieties of apple you want, and, if you can, taste an apple from the variety before you buy it. You don't want to go to all the trouble and time of growing the tree and then find 5 years down the line that the fruit is not to your taste. Buy a few varieties of apple that fruit at different times. Buy from a real fruit nursery rather than a garden centre and choose trees that will grow to the size suitable for your space. Apple trees usually need to be pollinated by another tree, so make sure there's one nearby that flowers at approximately the same time. In apple-growing areas in England, the trees are still wassailed in the traditional manner to encourage them to crop well. This involves toasting them and leaving them cakes and cider as a gift at New Year, which sounds like fun.

Hedgerow jelly

Wild berries do not have a great deal of juice, but they do have lots of flavour. Apples have a mild flavour but a great deal of juice – and also pectin and acid, which are what sets the jelly. So we combine the two. I find the perfect ratio is 1 part berries to 3 parts sour green apples. The sourer the apples the better as these have the most acid and pectin. Makes about 4.5 kg (10 lb).

1 kg (2¼ lb) hedgerow berries (a mix of elderberry, blackberry, sloe, rosehip, haw, rowanberry, damson, etc., or any of these on its own)

Water

3 kg (6¾ lb) apples

Sugar

1 Place the wild fruit in a preserving pot and add enough water to just cover the fruit. Cook this over a medium heat until the fruit starts to soften (about 20 minutes).

2 Roughly chop the apples (don't peel or core them) and add to the pot with enough extra water to cover them.

3 Now cook it all up on a medium to high heat for about 40 minutes until the apples and wild fruit have gone to mush. Watch out for the apples swelling as they cook – they will try to push out of the pot. Keep pushing them back under the water with a wooden spoon.

4 Put the cooked fruit into a clean rinsed jelly bag and leave to drain above a bowl for at least an hour if not overnight.

5 Measure the amount of juice in the bowl. Put it into a preserving pan. It will be cloudy, but adding the sugar and heating will clear it.

6 Add 450 g (1 lb) of sugar for every 600 ml (1 pint) of juice. Stir the mixture over a medium heat until the sugar is dissolved. Turn up the heat to high and cook until it reaches setting point (see p. 192). Remove from the heat.

7 Pour into warm sterilised jars to within 6 mm (¼ inch) of the top, lid and seal.

Foraging 101

We start harvesting blackberries when they appear in late July and continue on until Halloween. We also pick crab apples, fraughans, rowanberries, rosehips, haws, sloes, elderberries, damsons and feral greengages. It can be hard to find crab apples. I start watching the hedges in springtime, looking for the blossoming trees. Come May, they are covered in a glorious mantle of pale pink flowers. Crab apples were often planted to show the boundaries of old townlands, so if you find one tree there are often more nearby. I make a note of where they are and go back again in the autumn. I also watch for the elders. In June, they are swathed in white blossoms and can be spotted quite a distance away. I pick some of the flowers, but I leave most for elderberries. Damsons and greengages were often used as hedging. Keep an eye out as an overgrown hedge could be filled with a plummy bounty. To find the best foraging, ask the locals, especially gardeners and people with an interest in wildlife. Often they will be happy to share their knowledge of where the best sloe patches are or the location of a hidden crab apple. Then again, they might want to guard their crop – I understand that too. There are a few things to remember:

- Pick fruit where there is no pollution or chemical spraying.
- Don't pick everything you see. Leave some for the wildlife and some to reseed. A good rule of thumb is to only pick a third.
- Ask permission before you go onto someone's land. Close gates after yourself, and watch out for livestock.
- Don't bring your dog on someone else's land.
- Bring a hooked stick with you for those out-of-reach branches.
- Bring a pair of secateurs to snip clusters of berries – you won't damage the tree that way.
- Make sure you pick what you mean to pick: get a good guide or learn from an experienced forager.

    If you picked more wild berries than you can use immediately, you can freeze them. When we were young, Mom used to pick hundreds of pounds of wild fruit every autumn and freeze it for later use.

Spiced apple and damson fruit leather

Fruit leathers (or fruit wind-ups) are thin, flexible sheets of dried fruit purée that look and feel like leather (hence the name). They have an intense fruit flavour and are great for snacks, delicious chopped in muesli and porridge or added to your winter crumbles and pies. You can make fruit leathers from any fruit: turn it into a smooth, thick purée, sweeten it, flavour it and then dry it. You can use either cooked or raw fruit. I usually use raw local honey to sweeten my leathers as this adds extra goodness to them, but you can use sugar, stevia, syrup – whatever you like. Fruit leathers will keep in an airtight container for at least 4 months. This recipe makes one sheet the size of a large baking tray (40×30 cm/16×12 inch).

450 g (1 lb) apples (preferably eating apples), roughly chopped

450 g (1 lb) damsons

150 ml (¼ pint) water

110–225 g (4–8 oz) raw honey

¼ tsp cinnamon

1 Place the fruit and water in a pot and cook until it is soft (about 25–30 minutes). Purée by passing it through a sieve or mouli. This removes the seeds, stones and skin.

2 Add half of the honey and the cinnamon. Taste it and add more honey if you feel it needs it. Damsons can be quite sour.

3 Spread a 6-mm (¼-inch) layer on a large baking sheet lined with parchment paper. Try to spread it as evenly as possible.

4 Place the baking sheet in a 50°C (120°F/Gas ⅛) oven (or as low as your oven will go) and let it dry until it peels off the paper easily but is still flexible enough to roll. Don't wait until it's brittle. This may take anything from 4 to 12 hours.

5 Remove from the parchment and either roll it up or cut it into shapes and then store it in a paper-lined, airtight tin.

Variations
Try spicy tomato with pepper, or apple and sage with smoked salt.

TIP: Fruit leather is a great way to use the fruit pulp left in the jelly bag after the juice has been drained off. Push the cooked fruit pulp through a sieve or mouli to remove any pieces of skin, stems or seeds. Sweeten and spice the resulting purée to taste and then proceed as above. (Don't use pulp that contains rosehips as they have hairs that can irritate the mouth and stomach.)

THIS WEEK
MADE LAST NIGHT
NEW SEASON
WINDFALL

APRON

Jars €4 3 for
The Green Apron
The Green Apron

BLOOD ORANGE
The Green Apron
Blood Orange Marmalade

GREEN APRON
Spicy Tomato + Charred Pepper

Apple butter

This is basically a smooth, stiff fruit jam. Spread it on hot buttered toast or scones, add to porridge, or eat with meats (especially pork) and cheeses. You can also use it as a delicious bottom layer in tarts or as a filling for cakes. Makes about 1.6 kg (3½ lb).

900 g (2 lb) cooking apples

300 ml (½ pint) water

Sugar

¼ tsp cinnamon

1 Chop the apples (skin, seeds, stems and all) and put in a preserving pan with the water. Cook over a medium heat until pulpy. Put the cooked pulp through a mouli to remove seeds and stems. This will produce a thick purée.

2 Weigh the purée and put it in a preserving pan. For every 450 g (1 lb) of purée, add 450 g (1 lb) of sugar.

3 Add the cinnamon and cook over a medium to high heat, stirring constantly (it will try to stick to the bottom of the pot) until it reaches setting point. It gets very thick and blurps all over the stove as it approaches this point so cover your arms and wear an oven mitt.

4 Pour into warm sterilised jars to within 6 mm (¼ inch) of the top, lid and seal.

Variations
Try other spices such as cloves, allspice or nutmeg.
Add lemon juice if the flavour needs to be sharpened. I sometimes add alcohol, such as apple schnapps. Add 1–2 tablespoons of alcohol for 450 g (1 lb) of fruit purée. I add it after the butter has reached setting point and just before I pour it into the jars.

TIP: Fruit butter is another great way to use up the leftover pulp from your jelly bag. Just purée the pulp, sieve it, weigh it, add sugar and cook it up. (Don't use pulp containing rosehips.)

Drunken pig in an orchard
(pork with cider, apples and sauerkraut)

This is adapted from Mollie Katzens' *The Enchanted Broccoli Forest*, a brilliant vegetarian cookbook I've had since college. I made Mollie's recipe, with its sauerkraut and cheesy appleyness, and added pork and cider. The cidered sauerkraut has to be tasted to be believed – so sweet and savoury. It tastes of autumn and orchards and bonfires. Serves 4–6.

---

4 large cooking apples (peeled, cored and cut into bite-sized pieces)

½ tsp ground cinnamon

Pinch of ground nutmeg

Salt

2 tbsp plain flour

2 tbsp slightly melted apple jelly or honey

100 g (3½ oz) walnuts (chopped and toasted)

200 g (7 oz) cheddar (grated)

110 g (4 oz) fresh breadcrumbs

900 ml (30 fl. oz) sauerkraut

2 medium onions (finely chopped)

2 tbsp butter

4 pork chops

150 ml (¼ pint) cider

1 tbsp wholegrain mustard or sweet yellow mustard

1 Butter a large casserole dish and set aside. Preheat the oven to 190°C (375°F/Gas 5).

2 Put the apples, spices, salt, flour and jelly (or honey) in a bowl and mix together. Set aside.

3 In a small bowl, mix the walnuts, half of the grated cheese and the breadcrumbs together. Set this aside.

4 Drain the sauerkraut in a colander and rinse it in water to ensure that all the vinegary liquid is gone. Set this aside too.

5 In a large frying pan, cook the chopped onions in the butter over a medium heat for about 5 minutes until they start to soften.

6 Add the pork chops and cook for about 5 minutes until they are starting to brown.

7 Now add the cider and mustard and cook until the chops are cooked through, which should take about another 5 minutes.

8 Add the sauerkraut to the frying pan and mix everything together, making sure the chops don't fall apart.

9 Cook the whole lot until the cider has all reduced down and there is no liquid left in the pan.

10 Put half the apple mixture on the bottom of the casserole. Cover this with the pork chops and half the sauerkraut. Sprinkle with the rest of the grated cheese. Put the rest of the apples on the cheese, then the rest of the sauerkraut, then top with the nutty breadcrumb mixture.

11 Bake covered (I use tinfoil) for 30 minutes, then uncover and bake for another 20 minutes.

Plum jam

The secret to making good plum jam is to cook the plums until the skins start to slip off and then add the sugar. This stops the skins from being hard but keeps enough firmness in the plums to make a chunky jam. This recipe works for all types of plum – from juicy, golden greengages to hedge damsons to plump purple Victorias.

2.7 kg (6 lb) plums

Juice of 2 lemons, plus 2 more if the plums are very ripe and sweet

600 ml (1 pint) water

2.7 kg (6 lb) sugar

TIP: If you want to make certain you've removed all the pits, count how many plums you put in the pot and make sure that the same number of pits come out.

1 Wash the plums and put them in a preserving pan with the lemon juice and water. Cook over a medium low heat until the skins start to slip off the flesh.

2 Add the sugar and mix thoroughly. The pits should all float to the surface and you can skim them off. Cook over a high heat until the jam reaches setting point (see p. 195).

3 Pour into warm sterilised jars to within 6 mm (¼ inch) of the top, lid and seal.

Variations
Try adding a teaspoon of cinnamon, star anise or ginger to the jam at the end of cooking for an extra-special flavour. For a savoury jam, add some dried chilli flakes. We mix 2 parts plum jam to 1 part soy sauce to make plum sauce for stir-fries, spring rolls and duck. You could add a wee bit of garlic, ginger and chilli to this.

Spiced apple and plum smoothie

This tastes like autumn in a glass: fruity, spicy and honeyed. If it is too thick for your taste, add liquid (milk, water, juice, kombucha, etc.). Serves 1.

1 medium eating apple (cored)

2 plums (stones removed)

1 cm (½ inch) fresh ginger (chopped)

1 tsp honey

200 ml (7 fl. oz) cold natural yogurt

1 Blend all the ingredients together until smooth.

Blackberry whiskey

Not just a tasty liqueur but medicinal as well – or so we tell ourselves. We make at least one batch a year and always have some stashed in the cupboard for tummy upsets and cold wintery nights. Use a decent mid-price whiskey as cheap supermarket whiskey is often flavoured and coloured with artificial additives. If you absolutely hate the taste of whiskey, use brandy or vodka instead. You must use sugar in this recipe as it acts as a preservative. Makes about 1 litre (1¾ pints).

450 g (1 lb) wild blackberries, straight from the bushes (make sure they are dry)

2 cm (1 inch) fresh ginger (grated)

700 ml (1¼ pints) whiskey

110–225 g (4–8 oz) sugar

1 Put the blackberries and ginger in a glass bowl or large jar and pour the whiskey over them.

2 Cover the bowl tightly (to prevent the alcohol evaporating) and leave for 3 weeks, stirring every few days. Try to not leave the berries in the whiskey for longer than 3 weeks as the seeds will impart bitterness.

3 Drain the whiskey from the berries and either discard the boozy berries, use them in a pie or eat them with ice cream.

4 Put the whiskey in a bottle and add the sugar to it. Swish it around to dissolve the sugar and then taste. Add more sugar if you feel it needs it – it should be quite sweet. Keep in a cool dark place. It should last for years in your cupboard.

End-of-garden chutney

This fruity autumn chutney is the perfect recipe for gardeners (or the lucky recipients of a gardener's bounty). You can adapt it to suit what you have available. If you've got a load of courgettes or a pile of green tomatoes that just won't ripen, use those. Just make sure to remove large seeds and hard peel. The allspice gives a spicy lift and enhances the fruitiness, while the mustard seeds add a savoury depth. It works very well with cheese, curries, pies, sandwiches and burgers and will keep for at least 6 months unopened. Makes about 5.8 kg (15 lb).

2.7 kg (6 lb) prepared fruit (marrow/courgette, plum, green tomato, pear, etc., chopped into small cubes)

900 g (2 lb) cored and peeled apples (diced)

900 g (2 lb) onion (chopped)

900 g (2 lb) brown sugar

3 tbsp whole yellow mustard seed

450 g (1 lb) sultanas

2 tbsp salt

2 tbsp allspice

1 tsp ginger powder

Pinch of cayenne pepper

1.2 l (2 pints) distilled malt vinegar

1   Place all the ingredients in a preserving pan and mix well.

2   Cook over a medium heat until it starts to boil, then turn it down and cook for about 2 hours until the fruit has all started to disintegrate, it has reduced by about one-third, it's hard to tell which fruit is which, and liquid has started to float on top.

3   Pour into warm sterilised jars to within 6 mm (¼ inch) of the top, lid and seal.

Variations
Add 2 teaspoons of ginger, a few cloves of garlic and 3 tablespoons of treacle to make the chutney more like an English-style brown pickle, absolutely perfect in cheese sandwiches or with a ploughman's lunch.

Blackberry jam

I can't think of anything that smells more like back-to-school time than blackberry jam cooking on the stove. It smells so rich and purple and sweet. The berries are plentiful enough in September that you can make jam, whereas the previous month they were treasured and kept for pies, pancakes and crumbles. I always add lemon to my blackberry jam to help it set, and the lemon flavour enhances the blackberries, especially cultivated ones. Makes 3.4 kg (7½ lb).

2 kg (4½ lb) blackberries

150 ml (¼ pint) water

2 lemons

2 kg (4½ lb) sugar

1 Put the blackberries, the water and the finely grated peel and juice of the lemons in a preserving pot.

2 Cook over a low heat until the blackberries soften and start to lose their shape.

3 Add the sugar, turn the heat up to full and boil for about 10 minutes until the jam reaches setting point (see p. 195).

4 Pour into warm sterilised jars to within 6 mm (¼ inch) of the top, lid and seal.

Sloe gin

Sloes, the fruit of the blackthorn tree, are mouthfurringly tart to eat when raw but make a delicious jelly and an even better gin. Rich and sweet and sour with an intense plum flavour, sloe gin is especially good on snowy winter days when a shot warms your frozen core. Traditionally, sloes are picked after the first frost: the frost concentrates the sweetness and flavour and also helps break down the skin so the gin can penetrate it (otherwise you have to prick the skin with a darning needle). I pick the berries in September or October, as soon as they are ripe, and bung them in the freezer for a few days to fake the frost. Sloes need a lot of sugar to make them palatable, but the end result is delicious. Use good gin. If it's not good enough to drink on its own, you don't want to have it in your sloe gin.

---

450 g (1 lb) sloes (washed)

280 g (10 oz) sugar

700 ml (1¼ pint) gin

1 Put the sloes in a large glass jar. Cover with the sugar and then pour in the gin. Put the lid on and shake.

2 Leave the jar sitting on the counter (to remind you it's there and that it needs regular attention) and watch the magic happen. The sugar starts to turn purple, and the liquid slowly gains a red tint.

3 Shake the jar every time you notice it (at least twice a day) until the sugar has all dissolved. This should take about a week.

4 Leave the jar to sit in a cool, dry place for at least 8 weeks, or as long as you can stand, shaking once or twice a week. I usually wait until just before Christmas to decant it.

5 Strain out the fruit, taste and add more sugar if necessary. Put the finished gin into bottles.

Variations

Use vodka or white rum if you don't like the taste of gin. You can use other stone fruit, such as plums or damsons. I've had some lovely damson gin that my sister-in-law Rachel's mom made. Just use half the sugar that you use for the sloes. Try spicing the gin with cinnamon or allspice berries.

TIP: Once the gin is made, you will have all those lovely boozy sloes left over. Run them through a mouli and use the purée in desserts or with game.

Year's
End

Pumpkin pie

The first thing I ever grew in our Detroit backyard was pumpkin, and I still grow pumpkin every year. I use glow sticks in our jack-o'-lanterns instead of candles so they can still be used for cooking. It's hard to say exactly how much cooked pumpkin you will get from a raw pumpkin as they are all different sizes and densities. I cooked a medium-sized (1.1 kg/2½ lb) pumpkin for this and got just over 450 g (1 lb). Makes a 23-cm (9-inch) pie that serves 6–8.

425 g (15 oz) puréed pumpkin

225 g (8 oz) plain flour

110 g (4 oz) butter (chopped)

Pinch of salt

6 tbsp cold water

110 g (4 oz) brown sugar

½ tsp salt

1 tsp ground cinnamon

½ tsp ground ginger

¼ tsp ground nutmeg

Pinch of ground clove or allspice

3 eggs (lightly beaten)

300 ml (½ pint) milk

170 ml (6 fl. oz) evaporated milk

1 Preheat the oven to 200°C (400°F/Gas 6).

2 Cut the pumpkin into large pieces, leaving the skin on, and remove all the seeds and the fibre. Roast, skin side down, on a baking tray until soft, which should take about 40 minutes. Scoop the flesh away from the skin and let it drain in a colander until you have got as much liquid out as possible. (Some varieties can be very watery; conversely, some can be very dry.) Mash to make a purée.

3 Put the flour in a bowl and rub in the butter until it resembles fine breadcrumbs. Add the salt and stir through. Then add water, a tablespoon at a time, until the dough sticks together. You may not need to use it all. Knead it a few times and then cover it and put in the fridge to rest for at least 30 minutes.

4 Preheat the oven to 190°C (375°F/Gas 5).

5 Roll the pastry out on a lightly floured surface to about 3 mm (⅛ inch) thick. Line a 23-cm (9-inch) pie dish with the pastry and crimp the edges. Prick holes in the bottom and bake for 20 minutes. Remove from the oven and set to cool. Turn the oven up to 200°C (400°F/Gas 6).

6 In a large bowl, mix the pumpkin with the sugar, salt and spices. Gradually add in the eggs, milk and evaporated milk and mix thoroughly.

7 Pour the pumpkin mixture into the pie crust, put tin foil around the edges to stop them burning and cook for 40–5 minutes, until a knife inserted into the centre of the pie comes out clean.

Variations
You can use butternut squash, Hubbard squash or any orange winter squash.

SUGAR

1 c. bu
¼ c. si
2 t. va

Crea
incl
tho

PRESSED COOKIES

c. butter or margarine
1 c. sugar
1½ t. vanilla

Cream margarine, sugar, and vanilla
well. (Add tint if desired) Press onto ar
minutes. 4-5 dozen.

PUMPKIN COOKIE No. 1

1¼ c. brown sugar
½ c. shortening
2 beaten eggs
1½ c. pumpkin
1 t. vanilla
1 t. lemon extract
2½ c. flour

Cream together the first six
raisins and nuts. Combine
cookie sheet. 6 dozen.

54

½ t. salt
4 t. baking pow
½ t. ginger
½ t. nutmeg
c. seedless raisins
nuts

beat
sheet. Bake

Sift together
kin m

ents.
teasp

Pumpkin cookies

We ate a lot of these cookies as kids because when you grow a lot of pumpkins you need to eat a lot of pumpkin! This recipe is adapted from one of Bob Allison's cookbooks for *Ask Your Neighbour,* a long-running radio show in Michigan where people call in to share recipes and household hints. These cookies will completely change your idea of how pumpkin can taste. Instead of the traditional pumpkin-spice mix of cinnamon, nutmeg and cloves, the recipe uses lemon, nutmeg and ginger for a fresh and light taste. Makes 5–6 dozen.

200 g (7 oz) brown sugar

110 g (4 oz) soft butter

2 eggs (beaten)

425 g (15 oz) pumpkin (cooked and mashed – see p. 152)

1 tsp vanilla essence

1 lemon

340 g (12 oz) plain flour

½ tsp salt

4 tsp baking powder

¾ tsp ground ginger

½ tsp ground nutmeg

170 g (6 oz) raisins (or sultanas)

110 g (4 oz) walnuts (chopped)

1 Preheat the oven to 200°C (400°F/Gas 6) and grease a baking tray.

2 Put the sugar, butter, eggs, cooked and mashed pumpkin, vanilla essence and lemon juice and zest in a bowl and beat together until smooth.

3 Add the rest of the ingredients and mix thoroughly. It will be a thick, batter-like dough at this point.

4 Drop a teaspoonful at a time onto a greased baking tray, leaving room for the cookies to expand. (They usually double in size.)

5 Bake for 15 minutes until golden brown.

Variations
I use fresh, cooked pumpkin for these cookies but you can substitute canned pumpkin, butternut squash or any orange winter squash. Sprinkle a little brown sugar on each cookie for prettiness, but only if you are eating them immediately. The sugar melts into the cookie after a day or so.

Growing pumpkins

Pumpkins come in many shapes, colours and sizes. They need a small wheelbarrow-load of well-rotted manure for each plant and a sunny, sheltered site. Plant out after the last frost. Keep the plants well watered through the growing season and shelter them from frost if it arrives before they are ready for picking. They can be stored until about Easter in a frost-free shed.

Sneaky pumpkin soup

I have my friend Anna Marie to thank for this recipe. She discovered that kids would eat soup made with sweet orange vegetables (sweet potato, squash or pumpkin) if she added the magic ingredient: a couple of cans of tomatoes. It tastes like canned tomato soup, all sweet and yummy, and kids seem to like that. Mine request I make it once a week, and the leftover soup makes an excellent pasta sauce. I roast the pumpkin first as it gives a better depth of flavour, but you don't have to. Serve drizzled with cream or yogurt or sprinkled with grated cheese, with a nice crusty bread or savoury scones. Yum! Serves 6–7.

680 g (1½ lb) peeled, deseeded and chopped pumpkin – about 1 medium pumpkin

3 tbsp olive oil

3 medium onions (chopped)

2–4 cloves garlic (chopped)

1.2 l (2 pints) stock (vegetable or chicken)

2 (400 g) cans of tomatoes (or more to taste)

Salt and pepper

1 Preheat the oven to 200°C (400°F/Gas 6).

2 Place the pumpkin in a roasting tray and drizzle with 1 tablespoon of olive oil. Roast for about 40 minutes until nicely brown and soft.

3 In a large saucepan, fry the onions and garlic in the remaining 2 tablespoons of oil until soft and starting to caramelise.

4 Add the pumpkin, stock and tomatoes and cook for about 10 minutes on a medium heat.

5 Remove from the heat and blend to a smooth purée. Taste, and decide whether you need another can of tomatoes or a bit more water. Season with salt and pepper to taste and serve.

TIP: Roast the pumpkin seeds with a drizzle of oil and a sprinkle of salt for a moreish snack.

Partridge in a pear tree chutney

This chutney is our Christmas best-seller (after cranberry sauce, of course) and is an adaptation of one of Digby Law's fabulous recipes. I start making it as soon as the pears come into season in late autumn. It tastes like savoury mincemeat, all rich and nutty, and is great with cheese, cold meats and poultry. It will keep for at least 6 months unopened in a cool dry place. Makes about 6.8 kg (15 lb).

3 kg (6½ lb) firm pears (cored)

1 kg (2¼ lb) dates

1 kg (2¼ lb) raisins

3 tbsp salt

100 g (3½ oz) walnut pieces

Juice and grated peel of 1 large lemon

2.5 l (4½ pints) distilled malt vinegar

1 kg (2¼ lb) brown sugar

1 Finely chop the pears, dates and raisins. I use a food processor.

2 Put all the ingredients into a preserving pot and bring to the boil over a medium heat.

3 Lower the heat and simmer gently for 2–3 hours until it is thick and liquid begins to collect on top.

4 Pour into warm sterilised jars to within 6 mm (¼ inch) of the top, lid and seal.

Apricot, orange and almond preserve

This is so good I eat a half jar on one slice of toast. The apricots are rich and soft and sweet, the oranges add a fresh sharp flavour, and the almonds add crunch. It tastes like a summer holiday. It won an international Great Taste Award in 2012 as well as Gold at the 2012 Blas na hÉireann Awards. Hurray! I use dried apricots in the recipe so you can make it any time of the year. It will last for at least 6 months unopened (and about 5 minutes opened – you will eat it with a spoon straight out of the jar). Makes 4.5 kg (10 lb).

500 g (18 oz) dried apricots

3.4 l (6 pints) water

1 kg (2¼ lb) sweet oranges

4 medium lemons

2.7 kg (6 lb) sugar

100 g (3½ oz) flaked almonds

1 Cut the apricots into quarters and put them in a preserving pan with the water. Leave them to soak for about an hour to plump them up.

2 Wash the oranges and lemons and cut them into quarters. Whizz them up in a food processor until they are in pea-sized pieces.

3 Add the citrus to the preserving pan and cook over a medium heat for about 1 hour or until the pieces of orange and lemon are tender and the apricots are soft and squishy. Stir occasionally to prevent it sticking.

4 Now add the sugar to the pan. Stir well and cook over a high heat for about half an hour until the preserve reaches setting point (see p. 196).

5 Remove from the heat and stir in the almonds. Leave to sit for 5 minutes. Stir again so the almonds are well distributed.

6 Pour into warm sterilised jars to within 6 mm (¼ inch) of the top, lid and seal.

Roast grapes

I have a grapevine in my polytunnel, and it produces about a large basket of grapes each year. Dad has a huge vine in his greenhouse, and it produces about three baskets each year – and it's a big basket. They are all ripe at the same time, which is far more than we can eat fresh. One year, I made grape and apple jelly, added grapes to chutneys and made grape juice, and we still had an awful lot left. Then someone suggested roasting them. So I gave it a try, and they are really, really good. How did we not know about this before? Roasting grapes concentrates all their flavour and sweetness into a small ball of juiciness that pops in your mouth. I like them as a savoury addition to a cheese platter, on cheese crostini or served on the side with poultry or pork. You can also try them stirred through rice pilafs and tagines.

A bunch of red grapes

Olive oil

Sea salt flakes

Sprig of fresh rosemary (roughly chopped)

1 Preheat the oven to 200°C (400°F/Gas 6).

2 Drizzle the grapes with olive oil and toss until they are completely coated.

3 Put them in an oven dish and sprinkle with a pinch of sea salt flakes and rosemary.

4 Bake for 20–30 minutes until they are wrinkled and starting to soften. Take them out and let them cool. Delicious.

Variations
Try adding other herbs, such as thyme, or some finely chopped garlic to the grapes as they are roasting. For sweet roasted grapes, use butter instead of olive oil and don't add the salt. Add sweet grapes to cobblers and other sweet baked dishes, or pair them with ice cream.

Growing grapes

Grapes can be grown against a warm south-facing wall, but to be sure of a good crop, grow them under cover. In Ireland, they grow best if their roots are outside and their trunk and branches are inside a polytunnel or greenhouse. The grape gets all the water it needs from the rain, and the rest of the vine is protected from the elements.

Sole Véronique

There's a shiny fish-shaped trophy somewhere in Mom's house. Back in the 1980s, the ICA ran a fish cookery competition in association with Bord Iascaigh Mhara (the Irish Fisheries Board), and Mom was a regional finalist with her Sole Véronique. Lightly poached fish, topped with mushrooms, onions and grapes, smothered in a cream sauce and covered in breadcrumbs. You can't beat that. I particularly like the pop of sweetness the grapes give to this smooth and rich bake. Serve with a side salad or boiled new potatoes. Serves 2–3.

8 (500 g) sole fillets

Juice and zest of ½ lemon

1 small fresh bay leaf

Fresh thyme

Fresh parsley

Salt and pepper

300 ml (½ pint) water

225 g (½ lb) mushrooms (finely chopped)

1 medium onion (finely chopped)

180 g (6 oz) butter

110 g (4 oz) green grapes

30 g (1 oz) plain flour

170 ml (6 fl. oz) chicken stock

170 ml (6 fl. oz) cream

Fresh tarragon

140 g (5 oz) fresh breadcrumbs

1 Preheat the oven to 200°C (400°F/Gas 6).

2 Put the fish, the lemon zest and juice, the bay leaf, a small sprig of thyme, a small sprig of parsley, 1 teaspoon salt, ¼ teaspoon ground black pepper and the water into a medium-sized baking dish. Cover and bake for 10 minutes until the fish is no longer translucent. Drain off the cooking liquid and discard it. Set the fish aside.

3 Fry the mushrooms and onions in 60 g (2 oz) butter over a low heat until cooked through and the onions start to brown. Remove from the heat and set aside.

4 Wash the grapes, then halve and de-seed them. Set aside.

5 Melt 60 g (2 oz) butter over a low heat in a small saucepan, then stir in the flour. Cook this roux, stirring it constantly, until it is bubbly all over (about 2–3 minutes).

6 Add the stock and whisk it through the roux.

7 Now whisk the cream, 1 tsp finely chopped tarragon, 1 tsp finely chopped thyme and 1 tsp finely chopped parsley, a pinch of ground black pepper and ¼ teaspoon salt into the sauce. It should look like thick custard. It will taste a bit salty, but it all blends together at the end. Set aside.

8 Melt 60 g (2 oz) butter and stir the breadcrumbs through it. Set aside.

9 Now, spread the mushroom and onion mixture over the fish and then sprinkle with the grape halves. Slowly pour the sauce across this and then top with the buttered breadcrumbs.

10 Bake at 160°C (325°F/Gas 3) for 25 minutes or until the top is golden.

Bircher muesli (overnight oats)

This is my most favourite healthful breakfast ever. Making it involves soaking porridge oats and fruit in a liquid until the oats are soft and then adding tasty crunchiness and berries just before eating. It tastes like an apple strudel in a bowl. It will keep in the fridge for 4 days. If you pack it into jars with lids, it makes a very handy on-the-go breakfast or lunch. This makes 1–2 servings.

90 g (3 oz) porridge oats

1 large apple or pear (skin on, grated)

375 ml (13 fl. oz) milk (or thin yogurt, or apple juice)

2 tbsp raisins or sultanas

1 tsp honey (optional)

¼ tsp cinnamon (optional)

TOPPINGS

Fresh sweet fruit

Toasted nuts

Granola

Yogurt

1 Mix all the ingredients (except the toppings) together in a bowl, cover and leave for a few hours or overnight until the oats are soft. I leave mine out on the counter overnight as I like to eat it at room temperature, but it can go into the fridge.

2 Once the oats are soft, it's ready to eat. Cover with its toppings and eat immediately.

Variations

This recipe invites tweaking, and the options are endless. Use whatever fresh fruit is in season to replace the apples and pears. Try a single type of fruit such as strawberries, peaches or cherries, or try flavour combinations like blueberry with a touch of lemon zest, blackberry and apple, strawberry and banana, cherry and almond. Use other dried fruit, such as goji berries, apricots, prunes, dates, dried pineapple or banana, and different seeds such as chia seeds, pecans, sunflower seeds and linseed. Use non-dairy milks such as almond milk or hazelnut milk. Add cacao nibs or grated dark chocolate. Or a spoon of peanut butter. Use your favourite home-made smoothie or herbal tea for the soaking liquid – or Greek-style yogurt (it will taste like cheesecake).

Banana and chocolate cake

This is another one of Mom's secret market recipes. It's not too plain and not too rich or sweet. It will hold for a long time and is easy to make. As a bonus, it's a great way to use up overripe bananas. It's important to mix the batter by hand as this gives a lovely texture. I use a good dark chocolate: 50 per cent or more. Makes a 23×13×8-cm (9×5×3-inch) loaf or about 18 buns. These will keep for 3 weeks in an airtight container.

170 g (6 oz) butter

225 g (8 oz) sugar

280 g (10 oz) plain flour

1½ tsp baking powder

½ tsp salt

½ tsp baking soda

3 eggs

225 g (8 oz) mashed bananas – about 2 bananas

½ tsp vanilla essence

60 g (2 oz) chocolate chips or pieces

1 Preheat the oven to 160°C (325°F/Gas 3) and line a 23×13×8-cm (9×5×3-inch) loaf tin with parchment paper or the bun tins with bun cases.

2 Melt the butter and put it in a large mixing bowl.

3 Add the sugar and mix well using a spoon.

4 Add the flour, baking powder, salt and baking soda and mix again. The mixture will look very crumbly and dry at this stage, but that's fine.

5 Beat the eggs and add to the mixing bowl with the bananas and vanilla essence and stir the whole lot together until everything is just combined and there are no large lumps. (Little lumps are fine.) Don't over-mix! Stir in the chocolate chips.

6 Put the batter into the lined loaf pans or bun cases. Bake for 1 hour (for a large cake) or 25–30 minutes (for little ones) until a skewer comes out clean.

TIP: Mash the bananas well before adding to the batter; otherwise you get lumps of soggy, cooked banana in the finished cake. Well-ripened bananas are ideal, but slightly underripe ones will work as long as they are mashed to a purée.

Boozy butterscotch bananas

This is our version of Bananas Foster, minus the flambé. We saw it being made on television and immediately had to try it. We've tweaked the recipe, and it's now my daughter Athene's favourite dessert (minus the alcohol). You don't have to use bananas; in fact, Athene prefers it with pears. You can use any reasonably solid sweet fruit like apples, peaches or pears – just peel the fruit before cooking. It's a simple, fast and delicious recipe. Caramelly, butterscotchy bananas with booze. Yum! Serves 2.

---

110 g (4 oz) butter

90 g (3 oz) brown sugar

4 bananas (peeled and sliced lengthwise in half)

1 tbsp whiskey, brandy or rum

1 Melt the butter in a frying pan over medium heat. Add the sugar and cook for about 4 minutes, stirring constantly, until the sugar melts. It will be all bubbly and golden. Watch out: it's crazy hot.

2 Add the banana to the butterscotch and cook until the bananas are warmed through and start to soften.

3 Pour in the booze, stir through and cook for about 30 seconds.

4 Remove from the heat and serve immediately – the butterscotch can start to split as soon as it comes off the heat. Eat it with vanilla ice cream.

Canadian butter tarts

Butter tarts are the quintessential Canadian pastry. They are so good they even have their own festivals. Dad first had these when he moved to Canada as a young man, and they are still his favourite tart. He introduced Mom to them, and she started baking them for us. Boy, am I glad because they are just so delicious. This is the recipe we've been using for the past 40 or so years. Be warned, they are very sweet, but they are very good and kind of addictive. They will keep for a few days in an airtight tin, but they won't last that long. I use home-made raisins when I have them, but only those made with seedless grapes. Use soft brown sugar because demerara makes the filling crunchy. This recipe makes 12–16 delicious tarts.

---

110 g (4 oz) butter

225 g (8 oz) plain flour

½ tsp salt

6 tbsp cold water

340 g (12 oz) soft light brown sugar

2 eggs (beaten)

30 g (1 oz) melted butter (slightly cooled)

1 tsp vanilla essence

1 tbsp cornflour

¼ tsp cinnamon

170 g (6 oz) raisins

1 Preheat the oven to 200°C (400°F/Gas 6).

2 Rub the butter into the flour until it resembles fine breadcrumbs and then mix in the salt. Add the cold water, a tablespoon at a time, mixing after each addition, until the pastry holds together. You may not need to use it all. Knead a few times until the pastry is smooth and then cover and put in the fridge to rest for at least 30 minutes.

3 Roll the pastry out on a lightly floured surface to about 3 mm (⅛ inch) thick. Cut into circles slightly larger than the holes in the bun tray and line the tray with them.

4 Whisk together the sugar, eggs, butter, vanilla essence, cornflour and cinnamon until the mixture is smooth, and then fold in the raisins.

5 Half fill the tart cases with this mixture. The raisins will try to settle on the bottom so give the mixture a stir before you scoop out the next bit.

6 Bake for 15–20 minutes until the filling is set and the pastry golden. Let cool for a few minutes before removing them from the tin onto a wire rack to finish cooling. (Don't cool them completely in the bun tin as they may stick when cold.)

Kiwi and green tea winter warmer smoothie

We often think of kiwi as a tropical fruit, but it grows very well in a temperate climate. We have two vines that have covered about 50 feet of our orchard wall, and they produce hundreds of fruit every year. Kiwis are late-ripening fruit, and ours often don't start to ripen until December. They keep quite well, up to 8 months in a dark cool shed, which is handy as our vines produce a lot. We eat them in desserts, salads and salsas and especially love them in smoothies. Serves 1.

2 tbsp porridge oats

300 ml (½ pint) freshly made green tea

2 kiwi fruit

1 banana

1 Pour the porridge oats into the green tea and leave to soak while you prepare the fruit.

2 Peel the kiwis and chop them roughly. (If you like the peel, leave it on.)

3 Peel the banana and cut it into chunks.

4 Blend everything together until smooth and serve.

Pineapple and rosemary upside-down cake

As kids, we used to make pineapple upside-down cake for Mom as her birthday cake. We always used canned pineapple because fresh ones were few and far between. However, now we can get fresh pineapples anywhere, anytime, so I decided to update our family recipe. I used fresh pineapple and paired it with fresh rosemary. They work very well together. The cake is sweet and caramelised and piney. This is more sophisticated than the old favourite and tastes like it should be in a fancy New York café. Serve with whipped cream or ice cream. Makes enough for 6–8 servings.

TOPPING

2 tbsp melted butter

90 g (3 oz) brown sugar

450 g (1 lb) prepared pineapple – about half a large pineapple

BATTER

200 g (7 oz) plain flour

2½ tsp baking powder

75 g (2½ oz) soft butter

140 g (5 oz) sugar

1 egg

1½ tsp vanilla essence

170 ml (6 fl. oz) milk

1 tsp fresh rosemary (chopped)

1 Preheat the oven to 180°C (350°F/Gas 4).

2 Start with the topping. Put the melted butter into a 23×5-cm (9×2-inch) round cake pan. Sprinkle the brown sugar across the butter and stir until mixed.

3 Peel and core the pineapple and cut into 6-mm (¼-inch) slices. Place the slices on the sugar and butter mixture in a single layer of concentric rings.

4 In a bowl, mix together all the batter ingredients except the rosemary until well combined. Stir in the chopped rosemary. Pour the batter across the top of the pineapple.

5 Bake for 40–5 minutes until dark golden brown and cooked through (check with a skewer). Remove from the oven and let sit for 10 minutes to cool – no longer or it will be hard to get the cake out of the pan.

6 Now for the fun part. Run a knife around the inside of the pan to loosen the cake. Place a large plate on top of the pan and flip the whole lot upside down. Tap the bottom of the pan until the cake comes away and lands on the plate. If there are any bits of pineapple left stuck to the inside, just fish them out and press into their spot on the top of the cake.

Variations

If you prefer a more basic cake, leave out the rosemary. Use canned pineapple if it's more convenient.

Mincemeat

I love mince pies, but I'm often disappointed by the ones I buy in the shops so I have to make my own. As soon as Halloween is over, I start thinking of Christmas and making the mincemeat. The alcohol is added to the mincemeat to preserve it; otherwise it will ferment. (I've seen a friend's ferment, and it popped the lids right off the jars!) I use whiskey in mine, but use whatever strong alcohol you have to hand. This is a variation on Mrs Beeton's recipe and makes about 1.8 kg (4 lb).

200 g (7 oz) raisins

200 g (7 oz) sultanas

200 g (7 oz) mixed peel

200 g (7 oz) dried apricots or dried figs or dried prunes or a mixture of them all

200 g (7 oz) cooking apple or pear (peeled, cored and roughly grated)

200 g (7 oz) vegetarian suet

200 g (7 oz) brown sugar

110 g (4 oz) almonds (flaked or blanched and roughly chopped)

60 g (2 oz) glacé cherries (chopped; optional)

60 g (2 oz) crystallized ginger (finely chopped)

¼ tsp cinnamon

¼ tsp mixed spice

Grated peel and juice of 2 lemons

Grated peel and juice of 1 large orange

300 ml (½ pint) whiskey, brandy, vodka or white rum

1 Roughly chop the raisins, sultanas, mixed peel and other dried fruit either in a food processor or on a chopping board and then place in a large bowl.

2 Add the rest of the ingredients and stir well.

3 Cover with cling film and leave in a cool place for at least 2 days, stirring a few times a day. Letting the mincemeat sit for a few days helps to prevent it fermenting.

4 At this stage, you can put the mincemeat into sterilised jars, lid and seal. It will hold for months like this. I usually don't bother – I put it all into a large food-storage container and leave it in the pantry as I'm going to be using it within a few weeks.

Variation
If you want to make a non-alcoholic mincemeat, use apple or orange juice instead of the booze and store the mincemeat in the fridge for up to 2 weeks or pop it in the freezer and use as needed.

Grandma's prune tarts (joulutorttu)

These are a traditional Christmas favourite that my Finnish grandmother made every year. She used to have to make double, as Grandpa loved them so much he ate the first batch as soon as it came out of the oven. The pastry is buttery and flaky, and the prunes are richly sweet. They are quite simple to make once you pick up the knack of folding the pastry – this looks much harder than it is. Makes 2 dozen.

PASTRY

480 g (17 oz) plain flour

1 tsp salt

1 tsp baking powder

2 tbsp sugar

340 g (12 oz) butter

1 egg yolk

250 ml (9 fl. oz) milk

FILLING

450 g (1 lb) pitted prunes

125 ml (4½ fl. oz) water

2 tbsp sugar (optional)

GLAZE

1 egg (beaten)

1 Sift together the flour, salt, baking powder and sugar into a large bowl and then rub in the butter in until it resembles breadcrumbs. Mix the egg yolk and milk together, add to the dry ingredients and stir until it makes a stiff batter/soft dough. At this stage, it's too sticky to work with, so cover the bowl and put it in the fridge for at least 2 hours. It's safe to leave it overnight, or even for a few days.

2 Cook the prunes with the water until they are soft. Vigorously stir the mixture with a spoon until the prunes have lost their shape and it's just one lovely gooey, pruney mush. Taste it to see if it needs sugar. If it does, mix it through now. Let cool completely before using (or it will melt the pastry).

3 Preheat the oven to 190°C (375°F/Gas 5).

4 Take the dough out of the fridge and roll it out on a lightly floured surface to about 3 mm (⅛ inch) thick. Cut it into about 2 dozen 4-inch squares and make diagonal cuts from the corners halfway into the centre.

5 Put a teaspoonful of prune filling in the centre of each square and fold the pastry corners to make a windmill shape. For an added finishing touch, brush the finished tarts with a beaten egg before baking.

6 Place the tarts on a baking tray and bake for around 15 minutes, until risen and golden brown. Remove from the oven and let cool on the tray for a few minutes, then remove to a wire rack to finish cooling.

Variation

Make these tarts with stiff fruit jam or fruit butter instead of prunes.

Grapefruit and cranberry marmalade

We make this marmalade in December, as soon as the cranberries start to come in to season. The cranberries turn the marmalade pink and make it extra tangy. (I do like a sharp marmalade.) If you can't find ruby grapefruit, use regular yellow. Makes 4.5 kg (10 lb).

3 ruby grapefruit

4 lemons

3.4 l (6 pints) water

170 g (6 oz) cranberries (fresh or frozen)

2.7 kg (6 lb) sugar

1 Wash the grapefruit and lemons, cut into quarters and process until they are in pea-sized pieces.

2 Place the chopped citrus in a preserving pan with the water and the cranberries and cook at medium to high heat, uncovered, until the citrus peel softens and smooshes to tiny pieces between your fingers and all the cranberries have popped.

3 Add the sugar and stir through. Cook on high heat until the marmalade reaches setting point (see p. 196).

4 Pour into warm sterilised jars to within 6 mm (¼ inch) of the top, lid and seal.

Cranberry sauce

We sell hundreds of jars of this every Christmas, so it must be good! It isn't just for turkey: we serve it with cheese and pâté, and I use it when cooking chicken, pork and sausages. This is a fast-cooked preserve so we usually recommend a shelf life of 2 months. Makes approximately 2.3 kg (5 lb).

1 kg (2¼ lb) washed cranberries

1 orange

1 l (1¾ pint) water

1 kg (2¼ lb) sugar

1 Place the cranberries in a preserving pan. Add the zest and juice of the orange and the water and cook uncovered over a medium heat until the skin of a cranberry smooshes to tiny pieces between your fingers.

2 Add the sugar and cook over a high heat for about 10 minutes. Remove from the heat as soon as it starts to set. Don't overcook it. Nobody wants a hard cranberry sauce.

3 Pour into warm sterilised jars to within 6 mm (¼ inch) of the top, lid and seal.

Variations
For a richer sauce, replace half the water with port. You can also add spices such as mace, cinnamon and allspice.

Cranberry cocktail

This is a great Christmas cocktail. It's so nice you may use up all your cranberry sauce and have none left for the turkey leftovers. Oh no! Makes one cocktail.

2 tbsp cranberry sauce

30 ml (1 fl. oz) vodka

30 ml (1 fl. oz) freshly squeezed orange juice

Ice cubes

60 ml (2 fl. oz) soda water

1 Muddle the cranberry sauce with the vodka.

2 Add the orange juice and a few ice cubes.

3 Top with the soda water.

Gifts

Food makes a great gift, and home-made food is even better. As I usually give food gifts to my friends and family, I gather bits and bobs all through the year so I can dress up the plain jars and bottles and present them well. I keep an eye out for other things I can use for labelling like fancy paper, chalk labels and paper tags. Place a paper doily, a circle of pretty paper, or a circle of nice fabric on top of a jar and hold it in place with a large rubber band (use a large one as small ones tear the doily). Then wrap rick rack, ribbon or twine over the rubber band to hide it. Simple, pretty and fast.

You can buy jute presentation bags. They look great, and all you do is pop in the jars or bottles and attach a label. Make a gift basket using a jar or bottle of your produce with something complementary – for example: chutney and some cheese, jam with a vintage knife and plate, or a bottle of home-made liqueur with shot glasses.

Preserving

Drying

Drying not only preserves fruit, it also intensifies the sweetness and flavour. I've dried oranges, nectarines, peaches, apples, tomatoes, raspberries, strawberries, blackcurrants, blackberries, courgettes, grapes and plums. I particularly love to dry grapes for raisins and plums for prunes to use in my baking. Throughout the harvest season, the kitchen always smells of warm, sweet fruitiness. Fruit is usually dried between 45°C (115°F) and 60°C (140°F). To use a regular oven, turn it to its lowest setting. If you have a range cooker, use the warming oven, provided its temperature is under 50°C (120°F), or leave the fruit on a rack on top of the range.

I core apples and slice them into rings, and I wedge nectarines, plums and peaches. I cut strawberries into quarters but leave raspberries, blackberries, currants and grapes whole. Large tomatoes can be cut into slices or pieces; I leave cherry tomatoes whole. I slice courgettes. Herbs, spices and salt can be added before you put the fruit in the oven or dehydrator. Salt and pepper on courgette slices is a must, as is cinnamon on apple slices.

Put a wire rack on a baking tray and a piece of parchment paper on top of that. Lay the prepared fruit on the parchment, skin side down, and put the whole lot into the oven. The rack allows the air to circulate underneath the fruit and speeds the drying process.

Different fruits have different drying times. Some have more moisture; others have denser flesh. The size of the pieces also affects the drying time. Apple rings can take up to 14 hours , strawberries anything up to 15, and courgettes can be ready in as little as 4 hours. The temperature and humidity in the drying area also affect drying time, so don't worry if it's taking longer than you thought.

Dry the fruit until it has become leathery, almost crisp. If you think it's ready, pop some into a transparent plastic bag and see if condensation appears within a few minutes. If no condensation appears, then it is dry. Otherwise, dry it for longer. Leave to cool for at least an hour and then pack into airtight containers. Your fruit should keep for at least 6 months.

Freezing

I freeze a lot of the seasonal fruit that I use in preserves as it gives me the flexibility to have fresh raspberry jam midwinter, cranberry sauce at Easter or elderberry jelly in the summer. I also freeze a lot of fresh fruit for using out of season in smoothies and in baking. Freezer space is valuable: there's no point freezing that slightly ooky punnet of pears that's been sitting on the table looking at you for the past week. You aren't going to want to eat them after they've been frozen either, so don't waste space. Only freeze good fresh fruit that you actually like.

Wash the fruit if needed. (Don't wash soft fruit like raspberries unnecessarily: it makes them watery.) Prepare as if you were going to use it immediately: hull strawberries, core pears, peel oranges, etc. Take out any unwanted seeds or pits and remove blemishes. Cut large fruit into bite-size pieces. Leave berries whole.

When I'm freezing fruit for smoothies or baking, I want it in separate pieces (not in one big block) so I can take only as much as I need. To do this, I spread the prepared fruit in a single layer on a baking tray and put this in the freezer. After a few hours, when the fruit is frozen through, I transfer it to freezer bags (I use heavy zip-lock freezer bags) or a freezer-proof storage container. When I'm freezing fruit for preserves, I don't need it to be loose so I just fill freezer bags with the fresh prepared fruit to the desired weight (1 or 2 kg), seal them and pop them in the freezer. It doesn't matter if it's a big lump as it will defrost in the preserving pan. I usually only freeze a single fruit at a time. I can always mix them together later.

You shouldn't need to wash wild fruit. Just be careful to pick clean, unblemished berries. I pick out any leaves and stems and put the whole fruits straight into freezer bags from my harvesting basket. I freeze wild fruit in 1 kg amounts as that suits my recipes.

Notes on preserving

- Always use a large pot when making your preserves as they tend to boil up quite high. Some even double.

- All of the preserve recipes are for decent-size batches of preserve. That's the amount that fits into a 9-l Maslin preserving pan, which is what I use. (I always figure that you should make as much as you can at a time.) Feel free to halve or even quarter the recipes, but note that they will take less time to cook.

- To check if fruit or peel has cooked long enough so you can add the sugar, take a berry or piece of peel out of the pot, let it cool on a saucer for a minute and then try to smoosh it between your thumb and forefinger – it should disintegrate between your fingers, leaving only tiny pieces. You must cook it until it's soft. Adding sugar hardens the fruit – so make sure it's well cooked or you have a jar of lumpy, nasty jam.

- After adding the sugar to jam, jelly or marmalade, always stir it in well before turning up the heat. Otherwise, the sugar may burn to the bottom of the pot and spoil the jam.

- Both the temperature and humidity of the day can affect your preserving. Your preserves may take a longer or shorter time to reach setting point and may make slightly more or less preserve. Always have 20 per cent more jars prepared than you think you'll need, just in case. However, if your recipe makes way more than you expected, you may not have cooked your preserve for long enough, and it may not keep well.

- The longer you cook a jam, jelly or marmalade, the stiffer it gets. If you like a very stiff preserve, feel free to cook it longer, but be aware you run the risk of either over-boiling it so it won't set, cooking off the delicate fruit flavours or burning it.

- Sterilise your jars as soon as your jam goes onto the stove to be sure they are ready by the time the jam reaches setting point. Have your lids washed and ready to be covered in boiling water as soon as the jam reaches setting point.

- A sugar foam often appears on the top of your jam, jelly or marmalade. Skim it off or stir it through the preserve at the end of the cooking.

- I usually give a 6-month keeping time for my preserves (unless otherwise stated); however, they may keep much longer. Chutneys especially can last for years. Use your judgement when using older preserves.

- Always cook preserves uncovered unless otherwise stated. The water needs to evaporate out or the preserve won't keep well.

- Sugar and vinegar are preservatives. They are what gives your preserve a decent shelf life. Do not adjust the amounts of sugar and vinegar in the recipes or they wont keep.

Preserving equipment

Bowls: I use plastic or stainless-steel bowls in various sizes. You will drop things, and this way nothing will break.

Chopping board: I use a beechwood board from IKEA. No need to be fancy.

Colander: Used for draining the washed fruit. I have a stainless-steel one.

Food processor: My food processor is my favourite kitchen toy. You don't need one for making jams and jellies, but making marmalades and chutneys would be drudgery without one. It doesn't have to be very big. Mine is only a 2-litre. Buy the best you can afford. I've been using my Braun constantly for 15 years.

Jars and bottles: I use new glass jars and bottles because I sell my preserves. Use recycled jars by all means, just make sure they are very clean.

Jelly bag: Use a thick cotton calico jelly bag. I often see cheesecloth bags, but the jelly doesn't come out very clear from those.

Jugs: I usually use plastic measuring jugs to measure liquid and to pour my jam into pots. If you drop a plastic jug into your pot of jam, it won't break, but a glass one will, and all your lovely jam will have to be thrown out.

Knife: Get a good paring knife and a good chopping knife. Keep them sharp. Blunt knives are dangerous.

Labels: Always have labels on hand to put on your preserves as soon as they are cool. Otherwise, you end up with a pantry full of mystery jars.

Lids: I use new, metal, vinegar-proof lids on all my preserves. I would advise trying to get new lids even if you are using recycled jars. If you simply must use old lids, check that they are undamaged and not rusty, wash them well and then boil them in a pot of water for 10 minutes before using. If you don't have metal lids, use the old-fashioned wax and cellophane lids. Be aware that they allow the preserve to dry out slightly after a time. You also have to cook the jam until it's very well set so it doesn't spill out of the jar if it tips over. That's stiffer than I like my jam.

Mouli: A mouli is a French kitchen utensil used to purée food. I use it to purée fruit for leathers and butters. It's much handier than trying to force stuff through a sieve. You can buy one in a good kitchen shop or online. Get a plastic one rather than metal as it's more comfortable in your hand.

Pestle and mortar or coffee grinder: Used for grinding or cracking whole spices.

Potato masher: I use a stainless-steel potato masher to smoosh berries when I'm making some of the jellies or jams.

Preserving pan/pot: Use a large, heavy-bottomed stainless-steel pot for your preserving. Either buy a special preserving pot, which is wider at the top than at the base (to allow the preserve to boil up without boiling over) or use a large stock pot. I use both. Don't use an enamelled pot like a Le Creuset. The hot sugary jam reaches a temperature that can damage the enamel. (I wrecked my large Le Creuset pot and had to throw it out.)

Scale: I use a regular kitchen scale to weigh all my ingredients.

Spoons: I use wooden spoons in various sizes.

Sieve: If you don't have a mouli, you will need to use a sieve to remove any bits of seeds and skin from your fruit purée. Buy a nylon/plastic one. Metal ones rust.

Sterilising

STERILISING JARS

1 Carefully check the jars for flaws. Look for cracks and chips – often the rim can be slightly damaged. Discard any damaged glass.

2 Wash well in hot soapy water. Rinse and leave to drain.

3 Cover a baking tray with 4–5 layers of newspaper and place the jars upside down on the paper. It doesn't matter if the paper gets a bit wet from drips – it will dry in the oven.

4 Preheat the oven to 150°C (300°F/Gas 2), then put the tray in for 10–15 minutes or until the jars are completely dry. Large quantities will take longer to dry (20–30 minutes).

5 Turn the oven off and leave the jars in there until just before you need them. The jars should be warm when you pour the preserve into them. If you put hot jam into a cold jar, the glass will break.

STERILISING BOTTLES

Use the same method to sterilise bottles.

STERILISING LIDS

Prepare the lids just before you need them as damp lids can turn rusty very quickly – and I mean within an hour. Sterilise the lids as soon as the preserve has reached setting point.

1 Check the lids: look for rust or dents and discard any damaged ones.

2 Wash lids in hot soapy water and rinse well.

3 Put them in a clean bowl and cover with boiling water.

4 Drain the lids on clean paper towelling or a tea towel.

5 Dry the lids with clean paper towels just as you put them onto the jars. Putting the lids on the jars while the lids are still warm from the water helps them seal better to the jars, so put them on as quickly as possible.

TIP: Here's a useful tip I learned from another jam-maker. This is only for when you are using solid metal lids. After you put the lids on the jars and seal them tightly, carefully tip them upside down for a second so the hot preserve resterilises the inside of the lid. (This is to make super-sure that you won't get mould growth on the top of the preserve.) Use a tea towel to protect your hand from the heat. Make sure you've the lid on tight or you will get a jam-scalded hand. I've had it happen to me a few times when I wasn't paying enough attention. Be very careful! You can skip this step: most preserves will be fine without doing it.

Safety

Be very careful when working with hot preserves as they can give a nasty burn. Jars of jam are hot, and so are the lids. I've been making jam for a long time, and I still manage to burn myself occasionally.

- Have a cleared and uncluttered workspace for pouring jars.
- Have your jars and lids laid out ready before you move the preserving pan from the stove to the work surface and keep the pot well away from the edge.
- Protect your hands from the heat with a tea towel or something similar.
- Have a damp cloth ready to wipe up spills as quickly as possible – a sloppy workspace leads to an accident. If you spill anything on yourself, immediately stick that area under cold running water.
- I find it's best to not wear shorts or sandals when preserving. Burnt toes aren't fun.
- Always use a large enough pot for cooking your preserves. Jelly, jam and marmalade boil up quite high. You don't want them boiling over, all over you and your stove top.

Jellies

The difference between jam and jelly is that jam is made from the whole fruit (including its seeds and skin) and jelly has had all the bits taken out so that it's clear. A good jelly should be clear enough that you can read through a jar. Good jelly bags are made from very thick cotton (so thick you can't even see through it) that filters out every tiny bit of fruit. I see people using muslin, cheesecloth and even pillowcases for straining their jelly. That does get out most of the pulp, but not enough for a perfectly clear jelly. Cloudy jelly will keep perfectly well; it's just not as pretty. Always rinse your jelly bag before using to help the juice flow through easily. The fruit pulp left after the jelly is drained still has flavour and can be used for other things. I purée and sieve it and use it for pies, tarts and also for making fruit leathers and butters. (Do not use leftover fruit pulp that contains rosehip as there are hairs in the rosehips that will irritate your throat and stomach.)

Apart from slathering jelly on my toast and scones, I also add it to my porridge, sweeten tea and make breakfast smoothies with it. I use it in sandwiches, such as the classics peanut butter and jelly and cheese and ham. I serve it with pâté. I glaze meat and vegetables with it: the jelly caramelises and gives the most wonderful flavour. I also serve it on the side with roast meat – think of the classic roast lamb with mint jelly. Goose and quince jelly is another deliciously perfect combination. Jelly gives an extra layer of flavour to gravies and casseroles. It's the 'secret ingredient' in barbeque sauce. Layer it in the bottom of your pies and tarts or make jam tarts and Batley cake with it. Use melted jelly to glaze chilled fruit tarts.

STEPS IN MAKING JELLY

1 Prepare fruit. Wash and chop if needed. Put into a preserving pan with just enough water to cover the fruit completely.

2 Cook on a medium to high heat until the flesh is soft. The fruit will swell and push up the sides of the pot – keep pushing it down.

3 Put the cooked fruit into a jelly bag and hang over a large bowl to drain for at least an hour if not overnight. Do not squeeze the bag.

4 Measure the juice and put it into a clean preserving pan. Add 450 g (1 lb) sugar for every 600 ml (1 pint) juice and stir through.

5 Cook the jelly on a high heat, stirring occasionally. To check for setting point, spoon a little of the boiling jelly onto a cold saucer. Let it cool, then push it with your finger. If it has reached setting point, the top of the blob should wrinkle. Jellies should have wrinkles about 2–3 mm high. If it's just barely wrinkling, boil it for a few more minutes and check again.

6 Remove the jelly from the heat and transfer to the work surface. Using a jug, scoop out the jelly and carefully pour into jars to within 6 mm (¼ inch) of the rim.

7 Wipe the rims clean with a damp paper towel to ensure a good seal between the jar and the lid.

8 Put the lids on the jars and tighten. Be careful: the jar and the lid are both hot. Leave to cool and then label.

Jams

When you are making jam, you need to cook the fruit until it is soft before adding sugar because sugar causes the fruit to harden. I've been given some very chewy blackcurrant jam where the sugar was added too early. The flavour was there, but the texture was unpleasant. Hard fruit also floats to the top of the jar. Don't use overripe fruit for jam as it won't set well and makes a poor jam. Use to make cordials, syrups, smoothies or puddings.

When mixing tough-skinned berries and soft berries in a jam, such as raspberry and blackcurrant or mixed summer berry, the tough berries need to be cooked first in water to soften the skins before the softer berries are added. Then both berries are cooked together until they are both soft before sugar is added.

Different fruits have different amounts of acid and pectin, both of which make jam set. For instance, apples are high in pectin but strawberries can be very low. You can buy bottles of pectin to add to your jam to make sure it sets, and you can also buy jam sugar with added pectin. I don't use either of these as I feel it changes the taste and affects the shelf life. I use lemons to increase the acid, and, if a fruit is very low in pectin, I add it to a high-pectin fruit to get the preserve to set.

STEPS IN MAKING JAM

1 Prepare the fruit. Wash, remove any blemishes and chop if required.

2 Put the fruit in the preserving pan and add any extra ingredients such as water or lemon juice.

3 Cook over a low heat, stirring occasionally, until the fruit is soft and the juices run.

4 Add the sugar to the pan and stir in well.

5 Raise the heat and cook the fruit and sugar over a high heat until the jam reaches setting point (around 20–40 minutes). Sometimes a sugar foam collects on top. Skim this off and either discard it, or, since it tastes just like the preserve (the texture is different), eat it on toast or use it in baking.

6 Test if the jam has reached setting point. Spoon a little onto a cold saucer. Let it cool and then push it with your finger. If it has reached setting point, the top of the blob of jam should wrinkle. I pot up raspberry and strawberry jam when it only just starts to wrinkle – I like it soft. For stiffer jams, like blackcurrant and gooseberry, I cook the jam until the wrinkles are 2–3 mm high.

7 Skim off any foam that has collected.

8 Carefully move the pan of hot jam to the work surface. Using a plastic jug, pour into warm sterilised jars to within 6 mm (¼ inch) of the top of the jar.

9 Wipe any splashes off the rims of the jars. This makes sure there is a good seal between the jar and the lid. I use paper towelling that has been dampened with boiling water.

10 Put the lids on the jars and tighten. Be careful: the jars and lids are hot. Protect your hands.

11 Leave the jars to cool and then label and store.

Marmalade

The traditional way to make marmalade involves chopping up the citrus fruit, soaking it overnight in water, cutting the peel into thin strips and removing the seeds. I've developed a much quicker method using modern tools – thank goodness for food processors. If you don't have a food processor, you will have to chop the fruit very finely by hand. Don't worry about leaving in the seeds. When you add the sugar they usually all float up to the top of the pot and you can skim them off. Marmalade is not just for toast. Use it in baking, as a marinade, to flavour hot whiskeys, as a glaze for chicken and sausages and in cocktails.

STEPS IN MAKING MARMALADE

1 Wash the fruit, remove blemishes and cut into halves or quarters.

2 Put the halved or quartered citrus, its peel and seeds still intact, into the food processor and process until the peel is reduced to pieces about 6 mm (¼ inch) in size. If you like bigger peel in your marmalade, don't process it for so long. And if you like very little peel, process it for longer. If the citrus mixture gets very stiff and thick in the processor, add about 300 ml (½ pint) water, taken from your measured cooking water, to loosen it.

3 Add the fruit and water to the preserving pot and stir well.

4 Cook over a high heat until the pieces of peel are soft and smoosh to tiny pieces between your fingers. (This can take up to an hour, depending on the size of your peel pieces.) Stir it every once in a while.

5 Add the sugar and stir in well.

6 Cook the fruit and sugar over a high heat until the marmalade reaches setting point (around 20–40 minutes), stirring occasionally.

7 Spoon a little of the boiling preserve onto a cold saucer. Let it cool and then push it with your finger. If it has reached setting point, the top of the blob of marmalade will wrinkle. Marmalades should have wrinkles at least 2–3 mm high. If it's just barely wrinkling, boil it for a few more minutes and check again.

8 Skim off any seeds that have floated to the top as well as any sugar foam. Either discard the foam or, since it tastes just like the preserve (just the texture is different), eat it on toast or use it in baking.

9 Carefully move the pan to the work surface. Using a plastic jug, scoop out the marmalade and pour into the warm sterilised jars to within 6 mm (¼ inch) of the top of the jar.

10 Wipe any drips off the rims of the jars to make sure there is a good seal between the jar and the lid. I use paper towelling that has been dampened with boiling water.

11 Put the lids on the jars and tighten. Be careful: the jars and lids are hot. Protect your hands.

12 Leave the jars to cool and then label and store.

Chutney

A chutney is a delicious sweet and sour savoury preserve. Made from a mixture of fruit and vegetables, vinegar, sugar and spices, it is an excellent condiment that can completely transform a dish. We use them with cheese, cold meats, pies, sausages, barbeques, casseroles and curries. I use distilled malt vinegar in all my chutneys as it has a neutral taste and colour, and I use demerara as the brown sugar because its flavour is mild. Always cook chutneys uncovered as the evaporation helps the thickening and preserving process. The flavour of the chutney often improves as it matures, but all my chutney recipes are ready to eat immediately.

STEPS IN MAKING CHUTNEY

1 Wash, chop and peel the fruit and vegetables.

2 Put the fruit, vegetables, sugar, vinegar and spices in a preserving pot.

3 Cook over a medium heat until the mixture comes to the boil, stirring occasionally.

4 Turn the heat down low and simmer for 1½–2 hours until the mixture is reduced by one-third, the fruit has disintegrated and liquid starts to settle on top. Stir occasionally to stop it sticking.

5 When the chutney is ready, remove the pot from the stove and put on the work surface.

6 Using a jug, scoop out the chutney and pour into warm sterilised jars to within 6 mm (¼ inch) of the top of the jar. Chutneys can be quite chunky in texture, so be careful as you pour.

7 Wipe any splashes off the rims of the jars with a dampened paper towel. Chutneys can splash a lot and be quite messy so this can take a while.

8 Put the lids on the jars and tighten. Be careful: the jars and lids are hot.

9 Leave to cool and then label.

Troubleshooting

SETTING
Jam, jelly or marmalade not setting hard.

Reasons
- The preserve wasn't cooked for long enough.
- There wasn't enough acid or pectin in the fruit.
- The fruit was overripe.
- The preserve was overcooked.

Solution
You can try to rescue the preserve by reboiling it with added lemon juice. Personally, I never bother. I find other ways to use it and share it out among my friends. You can also freeze it (in small batches) as it will not keep for very long.

MOULD
Mould on top of jam, jelly or marmalade.

Reasons
- The preserve was cooked for too short a time to evaporate off enough water, or the fruit was picked in wet weather and was swelled with rain. Both mean that there wasn't a high enough percentage of sugar in the finished jam to preserve it.
- The jars may have been sealed incorrectly.

Solution
Feed it to your compost heap or throw it in your brown bin. Don't eat mouldy jam.

FRUIT FLOATING
Fruit or peel floating to the top of the jar.

Reason
The fruit wasn't cooked for long enough before the sugar was added.

Solution
There's nothing you can do to fix this batch. Eat it up, and next time make sure the fruit is cooked enough before sugaring.

CLOUDY JELLY

Reasons
Small particles of fruit got through the jelly bag. Either the weave of the material is too open or you squeezed the bag as the fruit was draining to speed up the process.

Solution
There's nothing you can do to fix this batch except try and mask the cloudiness. When it happens to me (I am so impatient I sometimes squeeze), I add spices and pretend it was supposed to look like that. Get a better jelly bag (if that was the problem). Otherwise, restrain yourself from squeezing next time.

JAM FERMENTING

(It will be fizzy and smell odd. The lid may pop off.)

Reason

- The fruit was overripe.
- The fruit was wet.
- The preserve wasn't boiled to an adequate setting point.
- The preserve wasn't sealed correctly.

Solution

There's nothing to be done to save this batch. Feed it to the compost heap or throw it in your brown bin.

CHUTNEY FERMENTING

(It will be fizzy and smell odd. The lid may pop off.)

Reasons

- The chutney wasn't cooked for long enough to evaporate sufficient water to give the proper sugar–vinegar concentration in the preserve.
- The vinegar wasn't strong enough.
- Not enough vinegar was added.
- Not enough sugar was added.

Solution

Use bought vinegar, not home-made, unless you are sure of the strength. There's nothing that can be done to save this batch: compost it or throw it in your brown bin. Stick to the recipe, cook it for long enough, and don't change the sugar and vinegar amounts.

BURNT PRESERVES

Reasons

- Cooking heat was too high.
- It was left to cook for too long.
- The preserving pan was too light.

Solution

In our house, we call it 'caramelised' not 'burnt' until we are sure it can't be saved. This shows how often it happens here. Sometimes, slightly burnt marmalade can be rescued by adding a few tablespoons of treacle and some mixed spice to make a dark marmalade. You may be able to rescue slightly burnt jelly by adding lots of chilli flakes for a caramelly chilli jelly. Feed very burnt jelly to the compost or throw it in the brown bin. Slightly burnt chutney can sometimes be rescued by the addition of a few tablespoons of treacle and some mustard powder to make it a much stronger English-style chutney. I've also used smoked paprika, chilli and Worcestershire sauce to turn a slightly burnt tomato chutney into a smoky barbecue chutney. If the chutney is very burnt, just feed it to the compost heap or the brown bin.

Index

Note: References to recipe illustrations are indicated by italics.

Acknowledgements

I'd like to dedicate this book to my family. Most thanks go to my husband Mike for his patience and support (it's been a crazy year). I'd like to thank my kids Alex, Bella and Athene who helped develop some of the recipes and who were my recipe tasters/guinea pigs/minions. The girls did an amazing job helping to cook and style the food for the photographs. Thanks Mom and Dad for teaching me to grow my own food and to cook, and thanks for all the great recipes and help. And thanks to my siblings for the years of cooking together and sharing recipes.

Thanks to everyone who shared their recipes with me for this book: Anna Marie, Anne, Katrina, Nancy, Corrin, Cathy and, of course, my Grandma Minda. Thanks to Barry, who helped me tidy up the recipes and translate the American ones. Thanks to my father-in-law, Bob, who made me beautiful wooden boards for the photographs.

Thanks to Val for her wonderful photographs and for teaching us food styling. Thanks to all my family and friends who've put up with me monopolising the conversations for the past year with bookiness – and swiping their plates, jars and cutlery for photos. Thanks for your support guys. Thanks to Pia, Lena and Tony – my fruit-picking models.